D1625176

Praise for *Success from Anywhere*

"Your personal guide to unlock higher purpose and humor in yourself, your teams and in your organizations."
—Dr. Jennifer Aaker and Naomi Bagdonas,
Stanford Graduate School of Business Professors and
Best Selling Authors of *Humor, Seriously*

"Karen's superpowers lie equally in storytelling and strategy, as evidenced by this pager-turner, packed with advice. A must-read for organizations of all sizes."
—Coco Brown, founder and CEO of Athena Alliance

"The pandemic can be a powerful catalyst for us to redefine the game of life and the game of work so that everyone can have an equal opportunity to win. Karen Mangia provides us with an approach that will help all of us to succeed."
—John Hagel, founder and CEO of Beyond Our Edge

Success from Anywhere

Success
from
Anywhere

Create Your Own Future of Work
—— from the Inside Out ——

KAREN MANGIA
AUTHOR OF *WORKING FROM HOME*

WILEY

Published by John Wiley & Sons, Inc., Hoboken, New Jersey.
Published simultaneously in Canada.

For general information on our other products and services or for technical support, please contact our Customer Care Department within the United States at (800) 762-2974, outside the United States at (317) 572-3993 or fax (317) 572-4002.

Wiley publishes in a variety of print and electronic formats and by print-on-demand. Some material included with standard print versions of this book may not be included in e-books or in print-on-demand. If this book refers to media such as a CD or DVD that is not included in the version you purchased, you may download this material at http://booksupport.wiley.com. For more information about Wiley products, visit www.wiley.com.

Library of Congress Cataloging-in-Publication Data

Names: Mangia, Karen, 1975- author.
Title: Success from anywhere : create your own future of work
   from the inside out / Karen Mangia.
Description: Hoboken, New Jersey : Wiley, [2022] | Includes index.
Identifiers: LCCN 2021043683 (print) | LCCN 2021043684 (ebook) | ISBN
   9781119834625 (hardback) | ISBN 9781119834656 (adobe pdf) | ISBN
   9781119834649 (epub)
Subjects: LCSH: Success in business. | Flexible work arrangements.
Classification: LCC HF5386 .M3055 2022 (print) | LCC HF5386 (ebook) | DDC
   650.1—dc23
LC record available at https://lccn.loc.gov/2021043683
LC ebook record available at https://lccn.loc.gov/2021043684

Cover image: Bird and cage © francescoch / GettyImages
Cover design: Wiley

SKY10030145_100721

To my brother, Paul

Who teaches me each day how to enjoy playing the game

Contents.

About the Workbook

Thank you for purchasing *Success from Anywhere*.

We have created a Workbook to supplement your experience.

You may access the Workbook provided for your use by visiting: www.wiley.com\go\mangia\successfromanywhere.

(Password: Mangia123)

Foreword.

It's never too late to decide what you want to be when you grow up. I'm still deciding what that looks like every day. How about you?

When I retired from Monster.com in 2005, I had completed a 360-degree entrepreneurial experience: I had been the founder, the president, the CEO, the chairman, and even chief monster (which is a title I still hold to this day). During my career, I've started about a dozen companies. Now I work with Ray Dalio and the Principles organization, helping people to find and live the power of meaningful work and meaningful relationships. But I'm not done with my journey, and neither are you. In fact, when it comes to exploring success, our journey is always just beginning.

Because you can find success anywhere, if you understand how to turn work into play. I found both joy and success for my company when we jumped into Boston Harbor together. That's right. We were talking about team-building ideas and I didn't want to go bowling.

"Let's go jump in the ocean," I said. Do you think everyone started putting on their bathing suits?

No. No, they did not. But in the end we all did it – together.

From there, what was once a one-time dare became an annual tradition, "The Leap of Faith." And yes, I was the first to jump. Because that's what leaders do. Having a vision is great, but you've got to take action. You've got to be willing to take the leap.

But here's the crazy thing: the meetings we had after that shared experience off that pier each year are some of the most unforgettable moments I've ever had in business. Because we shared an adventure. We shared a choice to try something different. The shared experience was success, in and of itself. That shared experience is something I strive to find in every aspect of my life, whether it's at Burning Man creating and running my theme camp called Root Society, or while actively volunteering in my local community in Connecticut. That shared experience is where the magic is. And that experience is something I find every time I tell my stories with an audience, as a keynote speaker. We share, we laugh, and we learn together.

I wonder, what's the adventure you'd like to create for yourself, and your organization? What's that new experience that would make a meaningful difference in your career? Karen is here to help you seize your own spirit of adventure, and move towards new goals and new horizons. And she does it with these amazing stories—and practical exercises—that will inspire you to take action.

Which is great, because stories are better than jokes. I mean, if you tell a joke, people laugh but they don't do anything. It's a trap, actually. Because, after you tell a joke, now people are waiting to see if you know another joke. Laughter may be the best medicine but it doesn't necessarily transform lives or careers. (Unless you're a comedian, but that's not the point.) Stories invite us to share new perspectives, to create shared learnings, and to reimagine our own impact on the world. Stories create a dialogue, and encourage new points of view. Karen shares her stories—many of them just happen to be hilarious—in order to open up your own perspective.

Speaking of perspective, I remember when Richard Branson challenged me to break his world record. No, not for space flight. He dared me to break his world record for waterskiing behind a blimp. That's right – waterskiing behind a blimp is a real thing. Some people use boats; Sir Richard Branson uses blimps. He dared me and I said yes. The result? I am the Guinness World Record holder for waterskiing behind a blimp. I told you I wasn't sure what I wanted to be when I grew up. Each day I get to decide, and so do you.

On this particularly cold day in Panama City, Florida, I got up on my skis behind a 155-foot inflatable flying machine. After some failed attempts, I caught and held a long-roped handle—holding on for dear life—and I beat Sir Richard's record. I am still not a great water-skier. That's not the point of the story. The point of the story is that I said Yes. I said I would try. Karen explains similar experiences with these two words: "Why not?" I've discovered that those two words can change the game – change your future!

See, I saw a blimp as big, but not scary. Sort of a monster challenge (yes, I said it) that if you push through, the fear can really help you. And, in life, what happens when we see things as fun instead of scary? What changes when we find new ways to embrace adventure? When we face what others fear?

I've been running life and living businesses since I founded Monster in the '90s, and I've discovered something: Life is a game that's meant to be played full-out. Now, I'm living my principles – and helping others to find meaning and purpose at work. Because sharing ideas is sharing success. Karen's ideas will help you to discover success on your own terms, no matter where you are. Because it's never too late to be who you want to be.

The journey to success starts right now with Karen as your guide! Inside this book you will find the courage to try new things. To make new choices. And to access the success you deserve.

Jeff Taylor
lifelong entrepreneur
GM/chief customer officer at principles,
a Ray Dalio Company

Chapter 1.

A New Game in Town

"This is the real secret of life – to be completely engaged with what you are doing in the here and now. And instead of calling it work, realize it is play."

—Alan Watts, British philosopher

"My work is a game. A very serious game."

—M.C. Escher, artist

I love to win.

In a time before smartphones, before Super Mario Bros.™ started their family business, before Nintendo® made their Switch™, my brother and I were notorious gamers. We played old-school games that lasted for days. Board games. Card games. Puzzle games. Sometimes we even set up camp next to our games, with no screens or distractions to interrupt us. My brother would hunker down in his Hot Wheels sleeping bag. Mine was bright blue with a rainbow interior. I always kept a red plastic flashlight inside of my personal campsite – not because I was afraid of the dark, but because I wanted to keep a night watch over the game. And to make sure my brother was playing by the rules 24/7.

The day was built around the game. We curtailed the duration of breakfast and lunch to return to the game. Then we figured out how to sneak snacks upstairs so we could eat while we played the game. We skipped playing with friends to play the game. And we staged a united front with our parents to play the game: we didn't always like each other, but we were feverishly united in resisting anything that might pull us away from the game. Doctor visits. Dinner. Family time. Baths. Bedtime stories. We understood commitment. The game mattered most.

Sound familiar?

Sometimes seemingly arbitrary obligations – like school and homework – required us to play shorter-duration games. Since my brother is four years younger than me, I would defer to him to choose the game on "quick game days." He predictably returned with the same box.

A board game called Life.

In the Game of Life®, players travel through their lives looking for success. Throughout the process, you earn money, make investments, get married, have children, and retire.

As you spin the wheel and advance your Game of Life®, you encounter a series of crossroads. Take the short route and go directly to business and to a salary? Or take a detour to university and the long road to business and a career?

The strategy to win at the Game of Life® – by design – is to accumulate:

- Cars
- Cash
- Connections
- Collateral

No matter how you play the game, all of the players eventually reach the block on the board labeled in bright red: DAY OF RECKONING.

According to the rules on the box top, you must STOP in the DAY OF RECKONING SPACE.

Hey, guess where we all are right now?

The game of life no longer feels like child's play.

I've lived through the unintended implications of playing to win the game of life at all costs – and I'm not just talking about the flashlight next to my sleeping bag. I wrote about the high price I paid in my first book, *Success With Less* (http://bit.ly/successwithless). And then I took a look at how the game changed, in my second book, *Working from Home* (http://bit.ly/wfh-karenmangia).

The pandemic brought us all to a simultaneous stop: a full stop in a space called the Day of Reckoning. And what our collective Day of Reckoning revealed is a tally of who's winning and who's losing in life. In real terms. With real people. Real people we know. Real people we care about. Real people who we want to win. I'm talking about our families. Our friends. Our local business owners. Our frontline workers. Ourselves.

You're here because you like to win. Are you ready to play a new game – so that you can find the success that will determine your future?

You and I now have to make a big decision. Let's decide, right now, how we move forward from the Day of Reckoning. Let's discover how to get unstuck from the patterns of the past.

After all, if you're going to win at the game of life, you have to see new pathways and perspectives. Otherwise, you're just going to keep retracing the same steps.

This book is designed, specifically, so that you can see beyond your limits. From a place of personal awareness and redesign, a new kind of contribution emerges. Does your organization need a better hybrid work model, improved diversity, or greater presence in Europe? These kinds of organizational design decisions come from the people within the organization. Therefore, *Success from Anywhere* really starts with you.

In these pages, you will find an opportunity to begin again. A blueprint for creating the future – one person, and one organization, at a time.

In a post-pandemic era, each of us has a choice: a choice to design a new kind of game, regardless of how anyone else decides to design, play, or win their game. But wait a minute. Does that kind of flexibility sound too good to be true?

I still work in a huge corporation. I still have a boss. I still have deadlines. I still have meetings. But I designed a new game for myself with new rules and outcomes and measures of success.

No one else had to change their game design for me to change mine. Playing a game I can win means redefining what it means to win. And what I'm willing to do to win. Even if everyone else wants to play the same old game. Or play by someone else's rules.

My premise for you is a simple one:

WHAT WOULD HAPPEN IF
WE COULD CHANGE THE GAME OF LIFE TOGETHER?

I thought it was impossible. Until I met Fitch.

"I've got a dilemma," I told him as I adjusted my mask. "I keep thinking there must be a way for everyone to live and work better. These COVID days aren't going to last forever. Lots of people are burnt out. There's a lot of people who aren't being treated fairly. There's frustration for everybody," I said, looking at my shoes for inspiration. "I just don't know how. I feel stuck."

Fitch nodded his bushy head of hair. His bright blue eyes looked back at me, over his mask, with an unfiltered kindness and empathy. You know the friend who feels like family? That's Fitch. He's always on the lookout – keeping his eyes open for the next thing. That game-changing idea. That plan that we can all understand.

A slight breeze on the back patio brought the reminders of early fall in central Indiana. Rays of warm sunshine danced on our faces, as we sat in the big patio chairs on the new deck. Sunset would come soon. Sitting in the newly finished outdoor kitchen, we were pondering a way to make things better. Simple, right?

Fitch leaned forward. "I'm trying to do something with my new company," he explained. "Look at the swings in our backyard," he said, pointing to a large wooden playset that included monkey bars and a small fort up top. "I think *all kids should be able to play on a playground.*"

Fitch continued. "I wondered, 'How could I create a playground for every kid?'" That idea turned into a subscription candy service, where Fitch donates 10% of earnings to help pay for new swing sets on playgrounds.

Fitch laughed. What was so funny?

"I know the best way to get unstuck," he exclaimed as he rushed into the house, calling out to me over his shoulder. "Let's play a game!"

The Game of Life®?

He burst through the patio doors and laid something down on the patio table. What was he planning? I looked down and saw it: a silver pen on top of a simple white notepad, no bigger than a deck of playing cards.

Before I could ask questions, Fitch got down to business. He wielded the pen and paper like a master artist with a brush and canvas. A moment later, he revealed his masterpiece.

"Wow," I said, "What game is this?" I wasn't sure what the masterpiece was, exactly. Was Fitch going through his very own Blue Period, becoming a patio Picasso? Had he just invented his own alphabet, or was that a duck chasing a snowman? I was mystified – and intrigued.

"This is our game," he stepped back and pointed at the pad, using the pen like a laser pointer. "The game we are going to play together." He grinned, certain that he had solved the puzzle that I had yet to understand.

"What are the rules?" I asked. "How do you win? I'm not familiar with this game." The duck might be a rock. I couldn't be sure. I shifted forward in my seat to get a better view.

"It's simple," he explained. "Just roll the dice. Choose a path. Any path that looks good to you."

The master in the art of living makes little distinction between his [or her] work and his play, labor and leisure, mind and body, information and recreation, love and religion. [S]he hardly knows which is which. [S]he simply pursues a vision of excellence at whatever is being done, leaving others to decide whether it is working or playing. To the master, it is always both.

—James Michener, Pulitzer Prize–winning author of *Tales of the South Pacific* and 40 other books

An appearance from his co-CEO interrupted our pregame warm-up. Janna sat down cross-legged on the corner cushion. She flipped her stick-straight hair over her ears. She overheard the rules of the game. "I want to play, too!" she added.

I turned to Fitch. "If she joins, won't you need to change the game?"

"Nope," he replied without hesitation, as if he had already asked and answered the question in his own mind. Resolute, he continued, "I designed the game to accommodate everybody. To infinity. And there are just as many ways to win."

A powerful realization struck me. My long-standing belief was that a game is an experience to execute. Designed by someone else, with a fixed set of rules, and resulting in one winner. Unlike my game-time focus on execution, Fitch saw a game as an experience to create. Designed with all possible players in mind, with a flexible set of rules, and room for everybody to play.

Fitch had the power to invent the game. He didn't have to follow someone else's rules, because he tapped into the power of a beginner's mind. How did he do it? Well, it's easy for him – Fitch is five years old.

In addition to being a full-time kindergarten student, Fitch is also the founder and co-CEO of You've Got Candy (http://youvegotcandy.com). In front of him sat a blank sheet of paper – the beginnings of a new kind of game. He looked at it as an artist would:

- An artist knows that the blank page (or empty canvas) can become anything.
- An artist knows that any drawing can be changed, erased, or thrown out at any time.
- An artist knows how to step back and shape the picture to his or her liking.

Fitch wasn't following the rules. He was creating them. What was it that coach John Wooden said? "Make each day your masterpiece."

Ever the entrepreneur, Fitch saw an opportunity to create a new game of life. A game designed on a simple yet profound premise:

- Every player wants to win.
- Every player has the ability (the potential) to win.
- Every player must have equal opportunity to win.

- Every player is welcome in the game, and you don't have to "bet it all" (or lose everything) in order to play.

Five-year-old Fitch saw what we often miss:

winning is an outcome of how you design the game

And everyone can be successful by design.

Was this just freedom in a child's eyes? Because I can remember a lot of times in my career when I felt limited. Constrained. Burdened by culture and norms and accepted behaviors and everything else. But freedom is a state of mind, not a set of rules.

Rules always exist; take the law of gravity, for example. But *Success from Anywhere* isn't a rulebook. It's a tool kit. To help you play by your own rules.

In the following pages you will find stories that point towards an expansive perspective, no matter where you are in your career. We'll look at where the blueprint originates and how new ideas can be applied inside your organization. Because the person creating the blueprint for you is – wait for it – you.

What would happen if we could all take Fitch to work with us? I'm not talking about pulling this kid out of kindergarten.

I'm talking about using his ideas around a new game of life. How might we design the new world of work, the workplace, and the workforce differently? How might we redesign the role of work in our lives?

Does that idea make you a little uncomfortable? Does it make your boss, board, and customers uncomfortable? I hope so. I hope you have the courage to challenge the status quo, and play a new kind of game. They say there's nothing that can stop an idea whose time has come.

This pandemic took something from all of us. For some, it took everything. Now, I wonder: what will you take from this experience? Perhaps it's as simple as a pen and paper. And the simple decision that there's a new game in town.

Your game. You make the rules. You design your masterpiece. You create what's next. Are you ready to build that blueprint?

Hold on a minute, you might be thinking – how can I find this kind of "masterpiece" freedom? How is that possible, inside my law firm, or inside this engineering company, or inside my job search – where I can't seem to create much of anything? It may seem like the rules are set, the parameters are fixed, and your fate is sealed. I know.

I've experienced what it's like to feel trapped inside an organization. Working for a horrible boss. Unsupported by colleagues. Blocked by rules and fools, wondering where I lost my tools. Wondering why success was just a far-off concept, reserved for other players (not me). Making my own masterpiece wasn't something I could internalize – or act on. Lost and afraid in a game I never made – yes, I know the feeling! But I discovered a new way to play – and you can, too. You don't have to quit your job, destroy your mobile phone, or move into the woods in order to find new possibilities. You don't have to escape in order to create; you simply have to change your relationship to the game you're playing.

Every game has rules. Every game has a way of keeping score. Just because there are rules doesn't mean you can't play in a different way. Rules aren't the same as limitations – limitations are a state of mind. If that's still hard to see, let me just say: I know. I've been there.

But isn't it possible that a new perspective could help things open up for you, your company, and your career? Isn't it possible that you could take that blank page and create some new plays, inside your existing game? You know that new possibilities exist. How about a new playbook, in order to find them?

There's never just one way to WIN

If a player comes to her coach and says, "Coach, there's only one way to win! I'm trapped and I can only make it to the goal via this one way!" the coach would reply by sitting her down on the bench for an attitude adjustment. Because there's never just one way to win. Great players find every possible way to win – the way that the defense hasn't considered, the move that is improvised at the last minute, the creative decision that happens in a split second. The rules are there, but so is the ability to make a new move – if we allow ourselves to do so. In fact, in the game of life, winners find every possible way to win – and they are not afraid to try, to commit, to act with dedication towards new results. The game is still the game, but the player has discovered new options.

There's never just one way to win, as my brother often showed me. That's right. He's four years younger, but from time to time he would take me downtown. Game over. Ooh, I did not like those days, watching him end up with all the money in the Game of Life®. I remember being so mad! How could he beat me, when he was my little kid brother?

Turns out, creativity doesn't have an age limit. You can always figure out new ways to win, when you play full out. When you play with a blank page. When you aren't wrapped up in preconceptions or ideas about who you should be, it's easier to be who you are. And the game plan on your blank page can change – regardless of age, gender, or anything else.

We are living in a moment of opportunity. We don't have to get stuck on our "Day of Reckoning." Trapped in past perceptions and playbooks that no longer serve us, we will never create the future.

A powerful tool is available to all of us. A powerful tool to unlock our full human potential. A powerful tool to forever change the game of life. For the better. That tool?

Choice.

Choice moves us from past to present. Choice moves us from constrained to capable. Choice moves us from limited to limitless.

Often, it looks like the past determines the future. "Because of this," we tell ourselves, "I can't, or I won't, or it will never be different." But have you considered that looking at the past to create our potential is, by definition, a very limiting perspective? Isn't it time to take our creativity and potential out of quarantine? The past reminds us; it doesn't define us.

I am who I am because of my past, and in spite of it. The crazy thing about creating the future is this: the future never comes from the past. We can choose differently. We have the power of choice, and that power (like the pen in Fitch's hand) is always ready to create something new.

Our lives can be renewed at every level when we embrace the present moment as a limitless place. We activate our full potential – and the potential of those around us – by choosing expansiveness.

You may be feeling stuck right now. You may have resigned yourself to being stuck. You may be getting beat by your little brother, perhaps without even knowing it. Please consider these words: stay in the game.

Stuckness doesn't have to stick. Once you are aware of being stuck, you've taken the most important step to getting unstuck. Expanded awareness is where it all begins – seeing things in a new way is the first step towards progress.

We all want to lead a life in which our expectations, dreams, and inner potential get fulfilled. When you get unstuck, fulfillment is natural and effortless. You and I are fulfilled when we can be who we are meant to be.

Are you ready to live a limitless life? Are you ready to lead a limitless organization? Let's look in the direction of your potential, and change the game. First, you have to see the blank page in front of you. You aren't trapped in spring of 2020 anymore. Opportunities are all around us. Isn't that true? Acorns are turning into oak trees, powerful waves are crashing on the shore, new businesses are being funded right now, and people are finding new partnerships every minute. Step back and look at this game called life.

Are you playing to win? Or just making your next move based on the last one?

Limitless is a choice.

Three simple steps can help you to choose differently.

1. **Define:** What's the game you're playing right now? What does the "game of life" look like for you? How are you showing up, when it's game time?
2. **Design:** What new rules could you create for yourself? What old rules need to change? What plays could you run that you haven't considered before? What's that new design that would transform everything?
3. **Deliver:** Results come from action. What needs to be done, in order to raise your game? What's one thing you can commit to, right now, to get you closer to the game you want to play? Creative solutions are always available. Commit to finding them, right now, and you're on your way to delivering a new level of success.

Not sure how to win in the game of life? Pick up your pen. And make a new choice. This book will show you how.

Limitless is a choice

Chapter 2.
Beyond the Foundation

"Trust that little voice inside your head that says, 'Wouldn't it be interesting if. . . ?' And then: Do it."

—Duane Michals, American photographer

Dee makes everything effortless.

Impeccably dressed even for a grocery store run, my friend Dee brings undeniable class to everything she touches. Especially her home. She's the only person I know who can truly pull off white carpet in her house.

"I was outside doing some work on the landscaping," she tells me. I'm sitting in the passenger seat in her BMW convertible. Dee's hand is resting on top of the steering wheel, where a beautiful gold ring with a single shining pearl sits atop one of her manicured fingers. At a stoplight, she turns to me and says, "I was thinking of selling my place. That's when I found something that really scared me."

Her house was important to her. Dee raised her two daughters as a single mother in that house. Now it was time for a change. Like most people looking to sell, Dee wanted to make sure that she had everything in order. Somehow I could tell that it wasn't.

My friend looked over at me. She said she was putting the finishing touches on thousands of dollars' worth of landscaping work. A realtor herself, Dee knows the importance of curb appeal. Old trees were trimmed, new trees were planted. Bushes, too. Tulips. Hydrangeas. An elaborate array of springtime flowers surrounded the front porch and patio. The elegant ensemble of flora was blanketed with hundreds of pounds of deep, dark mulch.

"Behind one of the bushes, I happened to notice this crack," Dee explains. "As I got closer to it, I noticed the crack was bigger than I realized." She looked over at me. "The crack went all the way around most of my house."

I gasped.

Dee continued, "I contacted someone to come out and take a look at the foundation. The guy looked at it and said, 'Hey, no problem. We can patch the foundation. Shifting happens from time to time in the older homes. Not to worry, we've got this covered.'"

He gave her an estimate for the repairs. She considered the proposal. But she didn't take action. Why, I wondered?

Later, she explained, she was in her basement where she saw something she had never noticed before: a small puddle of water on the carpet, in one of the corners. Several feet above, inches from the ceiling, was a small crack, with tiny trickles of water seeping out of it. The drips of water from that one-inch crack were the source of the puddle – and much consternation. What was she going to do about that leak? Was it time to call the contractor and get started on the repairs?

"Nope," she said. "I wanted a second opinion."

The next contractor takes more time, both inside and outside of her house. He says, "I think we need to dig a little deeper."

Dee says, "How deep is deeper?"

The contractor replies, "Well, we really need to understand how much your house has settled. How pervasive are the cracks?"

Dee didn't know the answer, but she wanted him to find out. She told him, "Do what you've got to do."

He proceeded to come in and excavate every inch of that beautiful landscaping.

He pulled up the mulch. Broke up the bushes. The forsythia was forsaken. Daylilies? Destroyed. The workers put every ounce of dirt and flowers into a gigantic pile in the front lawn.

An unobstructed view revealed a series of cracks. Underneath all that curb appeal, something sinister was lurking.

Not just the one crack behind the bushes: dozens of cracks hidden beneath the once-beautiful landscaping.

"It's tempting to cover up the cracks," Dee explained to me. "Just coat them over or cover them up or put some flowers in front of them and hope no one notices." But what about your home inspection, or the disclosures for a new buyer?

"Well, I wasn't going to settle, basically. I had to pull everything away so that I could truly see what was going on at the foundation," Dee said. "I had to clear out everything that didn't matter: those bushes. Those tulips. That beautiful mulch." She takes a second to consider her initial investment. And how her investment had to change.

"I realized that my kids and my life and my entire world was built on something that was settling. And I'm at a point in my life where I'm not settling anymore. Even if it means taking a hard look – and believe me it wasn't easy to see those beautiful flowers roots-up in my front yard. But a hard look was what I needed. Because what I had wasn't working."

She was able to replant most of the big stuff, but the exquisitely planned pattern of flowers needed a redo. When the foundation was fixed, she was able to reimagine what her house could be, and that fresh start – without settling – led her to a powerful realization:

Dee had to dig deeper.

When she did, she discovered how deep the cracks in the foundation ran. What she saw and experienced led her to some powerful personal wisdom, not just a superficial fix. She called for a different kind of repair – a fresh look at the foundation.

When we all went home to work during the pandemic, we saw some cracks in the foundation. We experienced how work was working for us – or not. We recognized, individually and in our organizations, that there were leaks. Cracks. Settling.

Our values form the foundation of the future of work. Creating the *Success from Anywhere* blueprint means we have to have the courage to pull back the things that don't matter. Maybe even removing the pretty things that we've invested in, the niceties and the elegant facades that aren't serving us. They are hiding the cracks from us.

How much have you settled? What is it going to take to strengthen and to reinforce your foundation, so that your career (and your company) can create a solid foundation, not just a beautiful curb appeal for the marketplace?

When it comes to designing the future of work, the debate continues regarding working from home versus hybrid versus working in an office. There's also the element of the "third office" – that's the coffee shop, or the location for your offsite meeting. It's a third space where work gets done, a place that's neither your home nor your office. So the question rages: which space is the best place for work? What's the organizational design that's going to make the most sense?

The only person who can answer that question for you is you. The pandemic exposed some of the cracks in our foundations. I say "some of the cracks" because improvement is a journey, not a destination.

There's more to discover on the journey to your personal success. That's why a prescription for the perfect organizational design is about as useful as a football bat.

How about a blueprint that you build from the inside out? A game that you create, from a place of permission and choice? Now there's a way to make a fresh start. However, we must begin by looking at the foundation of any organization: the people inside it.

The key to designing the organization of the future is to start with one person at a time. *Success from Anywhere* is a personal playbook, where one size fits no one except you. Because you are the architect of your own game. You decide on your values. Not me. Not anyone else. And that ownership extends to your organization.

culture is built by the people inside it

Really, the most powerful discovery of this post-pandemic journey for me – what's been showing up for me in a powerful, attention-grabbing, impossible-to-ignore way – is that I've spent a lot of my life seeking on the outside what was missing on the inside.

Have you ever said, "If I only had _____, then I would be _____."

What's on your list?

Love? Acceptance? Worth? Kindness? Tenderness? Compassion? Balance? Wholeheartedness? Wholeness? Purpose? Passion? Value? Joy? Happiness?

And when parents and bosses and boyfriends couldn't give my list to me (because only we can give ourselves these feelings), I chased them harder. And when I didn't get what I was seeking, I got something else instead. I got sick. And being so sick became a source of shame.

In my thirties, I was gripped by a mysterious illness. My doctor was baffled about the cause. But the symptoms were not a riddle: no matter what I ate, I gained weight. I lost energy. I fought fatigue everywhere I went. Exercise and diet had no effect. I went from doctor to doctor – five in all – with no answers. A massive array of never-ending tests led nowhere. Meanwhile, my hair began to fall out. I developed what I thought was a tumor on my neck, and my eyes changed color! My experience isn't something that I would wish on anyone.

My life was built around making myself well – and it wasn't going very well. Since no one could tell me what was wrong, how could I know what to fix? For all the things I had accomplished and achieved, good health remained elusive. Good health – like personal success – was something reserved for other folks. Not me. I wasn't afraid of hard work or sacrifice. But no amount of effort would bear any kind of hopeful result. And I blamed myself for everything that had happened to me.

Because my personal illness was, in my mind, a weakness. My foundation wasn't cracked, it was crumbling. My identity was wrapped up inside a mysterious disease, with an unknown source, and constantly compounding implications.

Sound familiar? Can you relate?

Today, a crossroads around a health crisis is something we've all had to face. Fortunately, in my journey, I located the kind of help that I needed, and found the road to recovery. Today, that exploration of personal health and self-care continues – thanks to an unorthodox doc who brought me back to health. But I learned – and lived – the fact that disease can happen to you, regardless of lifestyle and choices. Illness doesn't care how much sleep you got or how many miles you did on the treadmill yesterday. Trust me, I've been there. I know what it's like to move through a personal health crisis and discover what's on the other side.

Here's what I've discovered about moving past a pandemic: I've found my answers inside of tap-dancing lessons.

Let me explain. As a child, I was unable to enroll in dance classes for a number of reasons. But as an adult, freed from old patterns and belief systems, I didn't need anyone's permission to experience (dare I say it?) some fun.

As an adult, I could give myself a different kind of experience. And so, I made a new choice.

I enrolled in a class at a dance studio where they cater to folks like me: absolute beginners. Never mind that most of these beginners are six years old; they also have classes for adults who want a fresh start. "What kind of tap classes do you offer?" I inquired. The school had a number of choices that could be a good fit for me. Their advice? Try them all.

So I did. And here's what I discovered:

- Permission is the path to possibility.
- Two words that invite fun into my world: "Why not?"
- Taking my four-year-old self to tap dancing has healed my soul.
- Being good or bad at something doesn't matter when you see the joy inside of an experience.

"If it ain't fun, you're doing it wrong."

—Fran Tarkenton, Hall of Fame quarterback
for the Minnesota Vikings

I'm still not very good at tap dancing, but I've never felt freer and more alive than I do when I'm in the middle of that experience. It's crazy! I never thought I would feel this way, but something inside me said, "Try it!" And guess what? When I allow myself to try something new, I discover more than just a snazzy shuffle or terrific time step.

I find myself.

And I find myself being more productive than ever. That's right. The key to productivity isn't a process, location, or structure. It's freedom.

The blueprint for the future of work – for your future success – isn't based purely on some organizational design or cultural construct. Does it seem like, "If we only had a better hybrid model for our team, then we would meet our fourth-quarter goals?" That kind of prescriptive reasoning seems comforting at first. Except for the fact that it doesn't work.

The right design for organizational success starts with the success of the people inside the organization. Success comes from the inside out!

Typically, if someone is explaining how "the answer" is an open floor plan, with more stand-up desks, you are talking to a furniture salesperson. If someone tells you that your culture needs to change, based on a six-step process, that consultant is about to sell you that six-step process. Do you see the cracks in that foundation? I have nothing to sell. But I do have a story to tell. And it's a story that centers on the nature of success.

There's a lot of bad advice out there, cloaking an agenda that's neither fun nor effective.

Success comes from the
INSIDE OUT

If someone else is giving you their blueprint for success, you're going to end up playing their game, not your own.

The source of success, I have discovered, comes when you access greater creativity and greater possibility than ever before. When you are free from the blanks and the biases and the barriers of the past, the thing that's waiting for you can be described very simply. I call it:

Joy.

What would it mean to you if you could bring joy to your work life? If that spreadsheet or whitepaper was an expression of something more than just obligation or a deliverable – but an extension of who you are? Your game, your rules: do you want to play?

What would happen to your performance, and to your organization, if a sense of fun and freedom and innovation were part of that thing called "work"?

Work might not even feel like work.

Your relationship to what you do would change. And when your relationship to something changes, the way you show up changes. Your identity changes.

Which is why you need to put on your tap shoes, right now.

I'm speaking metaphorically, of course.

So what's your "tap class"? Is it hiking the mountains in a national park? Playing softball again? Getting in the kitchen and making that recipe for chicken piccata? Booking a massage next Thursday?

No one knows better than you the things that will feed your soul. Don't believe me? Well, if somebody else's answers were going to work for you, they would have worked by now.

I don't know what your version of tap dancing is, but my strong suggestion is a simple one: get some new choreography, now. Take action to discover what you've been missing.

Don't be afraid to try a different tap class. Don't be afraid not to be good at something – you don't have to be an expert in order to experience joy, fulfillment, and personal freedom. Be an expert at living your best life, and finding the joy inside whatever it is that you are doing. Some joy is always available there, if you know where to look!

The counterintuitive thing is this: structure is not the source of success. Peak personal performance is not a prescription. The *Success from Anywhere* blueprint is something you create – if you're going to play to win!

A thoughtful connection to who you are is where we experience true success. Creating your own game, and playing it full out, is how you access new levels of performance.

Sure, structure always exists. The form and the physics and the guardrails are there for a reason. I often wish that gravity didn't exist, same with the amount of calories in heavy cream, but those limitations affect us all. Similarly, there are right and wrong ways to execute a shuffle ball change, customize software, grill salmon, or negotiate a raise.

But rather than focus on the tactics inside those games, for now let's concentrate on the player. Let's concentrate on helping you to enjoy making those moves work – or is that helping you to make work moves?

The answer is: both.

When we find time for ourselves, even in small daily choices, we create space for new ideas. It's counterintuitive, but the best way to produce powerful work is to find the freedom to play. To dance, if you will, in whatever shape that takes for you. Because, as we expand outside of the world of work, we increase our abilities inside of it.

When I'm dancing, deadlines and deliverables don't go away. But the way I show up inside of the workplace changes, because I reconnect with myself. My creativity. My potential. I play to see things in a new way. I learn some new choreography, and it reminds me that there are new moves I can make, in all aspects of my life.

When you are at a crossroads, feeling like peak performance is still in quarantine, here's how to break through. If you want the ability to begin again, consider your foundation. Consider what would bring you joy, and beat back burnout, so that you can put more play into your game.

When something feels out of alignment, I ask myself:

1. How did I/we get here?
2. How do I feel when I am here? (In this body. In this relationship. In this workplace. In this space. In this life.) I notice my experience.
3. How do I want to feel? (Healthy. Well. Successful. Happy. Joyful. Safe. Calm. Purposeful. Loved. Accepted. Seen. Heard.) It's possible to feel low and still perform high (I made President's Club the year I went through a divorce, for example). Success won't make you happy but being happy makes it easier to find success.
4. Is it possible to feel that way – to feel and to be at my best – **in a sustainable way** in my current circumstance/context?

(I created a vision for myself that says, "Honoring myself, I sustain radiant wellness." And I filter choices through whether they will honor me, sustain me, be sustainable, and contribute to my well-being.)

5. If yes, awesome! If not, what other choices might be available? (Create choices. Even if I don't love all the choices. Even if it feels the choices are big/scary/difficult, you might need to try a different dance class!) If it looks like there's only one choice – one way to play the game – chances are you are experiencing a misunderstanding. Other choices are always around; we just have to know where to look, and be willing to play, full out, when we discover them.

6. How would I feel if I operated from the belief that I have both the permission and the freedom to choose differently? (Maybe scared. Maybe uncertain. And also free. Perhaps even . . . empowered?) Look at your foundation, even if you have to pull back a few layers to really see it.

7. How could I feel more confident about making a different choice? (Support from others? New resources? New wisdom/leaders/guides? Remember, a Google search or YouTube video is rarely a good substitute for a powerful conversation. Who could you connect with, right now, to explore different choices?)

8. What would it take for me to commit to choose differently? (It wasn't easy to watch eight-year-olds who could tap dance better than me! But it's funny how we are all on different paths and different journeys. Is that a good thing or a bad thing? I see now that it's just a thing! I had to confront shame. When I did, when I really looked at where that

experience was coming from, I saw it for what it was: just a thought!)

9. What's the smallest step I could give myself permission to take/to make this choice? Or to progress toward my transformation? How would I reward myself for progress?

10. From there, I could look at my situation in a new way. I could forgive myself for previous choices that got me to a place (or kept me in a place) that no longer served me. After all, I was just doing the best I could at the time – and aren't we all? How I show up is my choice, not determined by anything other than how I choose to play the game. One small step at a time.

In my experience, it seems that every home construction project takes longer than expected. There are always unpredictable circumstances that show up – just like life. Dee's story reminds me that the unexpected is to be expected. We can always get a second opinion. We can always take time to have a conversation with someone – a coach, mentor, or trusted advisor – to open up new possibilities.

Sometimes, those possibilities point towards problems inside of our foundation. Transformation, whether personal or organizational, might not look like a fun game. So why would you play it?

Because you need a strong foundation.

Companies change, new competitors arrive, technology advances. Some organizational structures can't seem to adapt. The cracks continue. The leaks get worse. Can you find the courage to make a difficult choice? Dee did.

Do you value the outcome in a way that makes the effort worth the impact?

When we remember who we are, and what we want, the ability to take action increases. And so do our results. When Dee made a decision to get a second opinion, the game changed. When she decided to do what was needed, she was playing at a different level. She moved from intention to action. She uncovered her own personal commitment in the process.

Ideas without action are **just dreams**

Take action towards your goals. When Dee and I arrived at our destination, she let me know that she ended up selling her house for nearly 10% above asking price. She recouped the cost of both her landscaping and the foundation repair. True, her profit still wasn't as high as what she had hoped. But nobody was going to buy a house with a cracked foundation. That's not a commitment that anyone can afford to make, at any price.

Chapter 3.

The Stress-Free Experiment

"The more I want to get something done, the less I call it work."
—Richard Bach, author

"You've achieved success in your field when you don't know whether what you're doing is work or play."
—Warren Beatty, producer, writer, actor

The scientists staged an intervention.

Researchers at Stanford University asked a group of stressed-out college students to participate in an experiment over winter break. All of the students agreed to keep journals during the holiday. Easy, right? All you have to do is write.

But a select group of students were given a specific assignment. They were asked to write about their most important values, and how those values showed up in their daily activities.

The intervention had begun.

After analyzing thousands of journal pages, the scientists uncovered a new conclusion: writing about values helped these students to see new meaning in their lives. Students from the values group experienced feelings of greater confidence, resilience, and connection as they headed back to school. According to *The Upside of Stress* by Kelly McGonigal (Avery, 2016), the values group experienced better health than the control group (those participants just journaled about positive experiences over winter break). And get this: the students who experienced the most stress over break also experienced the most powerful outcomes from the values-based journaling!

Stressful and difficult situations were reframed for the students, via this experiment. Tough times became opportunities to reconnect with a source of strength, resilience, and ultimately, new ideas. That source? Their values.

What would it mean to you, and to your organization, if you could find a way to transform minor inconveniences into moments of meaning? Seeing your values in action is the first step in changing the game. Because writing about your values, the researchers concluded, transforms how you think about your experiences – not just the stressful ones.

Turns out, that kind of stress-free experiment is exactly what's needed to build your blueprint. Or to rebuild your foundation. Because your success isn't determined by me, your boss, or your board of directors. When you really get down to it, a future goal brought into the present moment is best identified as a value. So, getting clear on your values might just be the first step in reaching your goals! Science shows that values-based writing can make you more resourceful, more resilient, more compassionate – in other words, more prepared for the future of work.

In a similar intervention, but with a different test group, scientists discovered that this values-based affirmation exercise creates results that can be measured years later. That's right: people who wrote down how their values were reflected in everyday life showed positive effects even three years later

(Sherman et al., 2013, "Deflecting the Trajectory and Changing the Narrative," https://bit.ly/sfa-psych1).

Stanford psychologist Kelly McGonigal describes the impact this way:

> Writing about personal values makes people feel more powerful, in control, proud and strong. It also makes them feel more loving, connected, and empathetic toward others. It increases pain tolerance, enhances self-control, and reduces unhelpful rumination after a stressful experience.

Research from various experts shows that this values-based exercise – called a "self-affirmation" in many circles – can boost academic performance, improve both physical and mental health, improve problem-solving, increase collaboration at work, impact weight loss, alleviate drinking problems, change smoking habits, and more. (For more on the science, Kresswell et al., "Self-Affirmation Improves Problem-Solving under Stress," http://bit.ly/km-selfaffirmation2)

In describing what they call the "Psychology of Self-Defense: Self-Affirmation Theory" (https://bit.ly/sfa-psych2), psychologists Sherman and Cohen write, "When self-affirmed, individuals feel as though the task of proving their worth, both to themselves and to others, is 'settled.' As a consequence, they can focus on other salient [meaningful] demands in the situation beyond ego protection." In other words, connecting with your values helps you to move past your ego and find new solutions, by reducing defensiveness. Welcome to a scientific way to get out of your own way.

The blueprint begins with your values. Your values determine how you play the game. Your connection with your values determines how you show up. The shared values of an organization are the foundation of culture, performance, customer service, and branding. A powerful platform for change, yes?

Your values, extended over time, become your goals. Want to navigate through change, uncover the future of work, and build an organization that's ready for what's next?

Here's how to get started.

Game Changers.

THE STRESS-FREE EXPERIMENT

1. What are your personal values? Consider what you value most. Here are some words and phrases that might spark your imagination. What others could you add to this list?

VALUES

Family	Loyalty	Creativity
Freedom	Intelligence	Education
Security/safety	Connection	Respect

VALUES

Love	Diversity	Innovation
Openness	Generosity	Order
Religion	Finesse	Advancement
Joy/play	Forgiveness	Tact
Sports/athletics	Involvement	Wisdom
Nature/outdoor	Faith	Beauty
Adventure	Letting go	Caring
Kindness	Honesty	Education
Quality	Teamwork	Learning
Commonality	Career	Excellence
Contributing	Communication	Honor
Spiritualism	Entertaining	Wealth
Speed	Power	Affection
Cooperation	Patience	Insight
Encouragement	Pride in your work	Clarity
Consideration	Charisma	Humor
Leadership	Renewal	Home
Being true	Contentment	Friendship
Courage	Balance	Compassion
Fitness	Professionalism	Relationship
Knowledge	Patience	Change
Prosperity	Wellness	Finances
Gratitude	Grace	Endurance
Facilitation	Effectiveness	Fun
Fame	Justice	Appreciation
Willingness	Trusting your gut	Second chances
Hope	Getting the facts	Self-respect
Abundance	Reciprocity	Enjoyment

(Continued)

2. Choose one value that really stands out for you. Make sure it's something that you actually value, not something that you've seen in someone you admire, or a value (like "being on time") that's a label assigned to you by someone else. (It's great if you're punctual, and that others value your time management skills. But what do *you* value? Maybe there's something behind the fact that you show up on time – that's where you need to look! That impulse is the value behind the behavior). Do you value playing sports – or being good at sports? Notice the difference, observe your preferences, and get clear on what matters most to you.

3. Set a timer for 10 minutes and select one value.

4. Write a few sentences about why this value matters to you. Don't worry about sentence structure; make it a stream of consciousness. Just share what shows up and put it on the page; this isn't a grammar exercise! The power is not in your punctuation, I assure you.

5. Consider these phrases as prompts:
   - "These values are an important part of who I am."
   - "Here's how I see this value demonstrated in my life."

- "Here's how I saw this value show up today/yesterday/recently."
- Finally, consider this idea: "Here's how this value is going to help me to get through this next season/next quarter/next performance review/whatever is coming up next."

6. Share sentences about how you see your value(s) showing up, every day, and how your value(s) will help you to face the future.

Once you've completed the exercise with your top value, keep going. What's your next most important value? Repeat the exercise. Maybe you want to cover your top three or five values, in a deep dive. (That's what we do in my performance workshops and mastermind groups.) Look at what matters most to you. Then, if you're really committed to change, consider keeping a values journal, every day. Here's how that works:

When you find yourself connecting with your values, write it down. How do you see that value come to life? What actions or reactions show up, as evidence of that value?

there's no value judgment on your values

If these questions are difficult to explore, and you can't find ways that your values align with your actions, that's a very informative discovery. What do you make of it, when your life isn't allowing you to live in accordance with your values? If you can't find evidence of your values in your daily life, you've got to wonder why that is. (And if you want to take action on that discovery, stay tuned. There's more to follow.)

How do your values come into play, in the midst of difficulty, challenge, or conflict?

Remember, your values are unique to you. There is no value judgment on your values!

The choices you make must be your own. Otherwise, you'll end up conducting a stress-free experiment on behalf of your parents, your boss, or your ex-boyfriend. Let them do the work on their own!

In the middle of stress, go to your values. When confronted with uncertainty and change, go to your values. Getting defensive? Go to your values. And know that your values are simply an expression of preference, in a given moment (which is why it's useful to look at your values, and journal how you see your values showing up, on a daily basis).

Because your values can change. When they do, that doesn't necessarily mean you lack the courage of your convictions. The shift means that you are adaptable. Changing your mind is a part of being human, and seeing new options and alternatives is evidence of growth. Is the capacity for growth something that you value? That your organization values? Perhaps it's time for a values-based intervention, right now.

YOUR VALUES ARE SIMPLY AN EXPRESSION OF PREFERENCE, IN A GIVEN MOMENT

Before the pandemic, I was a road warrior. But travel wasn't a battle to be won; it was an experience to be savored. I traveled the world for my job, meeting people from Singapore to San Francisco. Then I would travel some more for myself, because I love it so much.

I wrote about my adventures on the Sydney Harbor Bridge in *Success With Less*. A realization on a Colorado mountainside made it into the final chapter in *Working from Home*. And an adventure in Amsterdam spurred several stories in *Listen Up!* But more than just what's inside my books, my global friendships have added untold chapters of richness to my global experience.

I've even met Her Majesty Queen Elizabeth II, in person. To say I value travel may be an understatement: travel has been a lifeline, and a super-important value for me.

Then the pandemic hit.

And my values had to shift. Can you relate?

Travel mattered to me, and it still does. But that value was reflected in different ways in recent days.

I still went to Malaysia, Scotland, Mexico, and many other places in 2020 . . . from the comfort of my home office. Maybe you did some screen-side traveling yourself, during the pandemic. I traveled from inside my kitchen, too. Whipping up dishes from India for the first time was an experience like "naan" other. New recipes lead me to new discoveries, while reminding me of friends and travels from days gone by. As I look to create the future of work, for myself, I wonder where my values might take me. Imagine if I wasn't able, or willing, to adapt?

In 2019, I earned lifetime platinum status at my preferred hotel chain. During the pandemic, I earned platinum status in my life. (The award ceremony was a small one, conducted at my all-inclusive resort, aka my living room.) But ultimately, the award that gave me my life back was much more satisfying than any free hotel breakfast I've ever had.

Adaptability isn't always easy, but it's always within reach. Because that's the way that we are all designed. We can adapt, and change, and find resilience in the most difficult of circumstances. If you're reading this, you've lived through one of the most challenging times in the last 100 years. But we've managed to make it through. We've shifted and survived. Now it's time to take our values and make a new future.

I could fill these pages with what the pandemic has taken from me. I'm sure you've got a few chapters that you could write as well. But the story that really matters is this: what are you going to take *from* the pandemic? What is your organization going to do, to rise above the stress of change, to transform into the place you know it can be?

The future isn't going to be built on regret, lost opportunity or past disappointments, even though those feelings are totally natural.

We've all been startled and stunned by the pandemic, each of us in our own unique ways. We have to answer the question of what's next. Is it more of the same – is that really what you're here for?

Kelly McGonigal explains in *The Upside of Stress*:

It's not uncommon to feel fear, shock, anger, guilt or sadness as you recover from a stressful experience. You may also feel relief, joy or gratitude. These emotions often coexist during the recovery period and are part of how the brain makes sense of the experience. They encourage you to reflect on what happened . . . . As your brain tries to process your experience, you may find yourself unable to stop thinking about what happened. You might feel the impulse to talk with someone about it, or pray about it.

The good news is that these feelings (and actions) are totally normal. McGonigal says that these experiences help create *plasticity*: the ability for our brains to adapt to change. Our brains can remodel themselves, it turns out, and the emotional process that we've all been through during the pandemic will lead us to create meaning from the experience. That's not a motivational speech; it's science!

In *Train Your Mind, Change Your Brain*, author Sharon Begley writes about a Spanish scientist – and Nobel Prize winner – who put forward a powerful idea: "In the adult centers the nerve paths are something fixed, ended and immutable." In other words, this guy said that the circuits of the adult brain are invariable and unchanging. According to Santiago Ramón y Cajal (the scientist), the adult brain was static. Hardwired. Permanently set. This fixed concept was heralded as groundbreaking at the time – which was 1913. Before penicillin was discovered. Neuroscience wasn't even a science yet. And his theory, presented as fact, was incorrect.

Edward Taub, a behavioral neuroscientist from the University of Alabama at Birmingham, introduced something called "constraint-induced movement therapy," or CI therapy. His treatment helps patients who have suffered the loss of motor functions due to a stroke, such as the loss of movement in a limb. Not only do his patients regain motor skills, but his work proves that the brain is capable of change. And, in some cases, complete rewiring.

In 1987, Taub and his colleagues began an unusual treatment for four stroke patients who were unable to move an affected arm. In a counterintuitive strategy, he had the patients wear a sling on their good arm for about 90% of their waking hours. The experiment lasted for two straight weeks.

During the two weeks, the patients played games. They held cards, threw balls, put pegs into a pegboard. They picked up sandwiches.

After just 10 days, the "useless" arms showed significant improvement. Patients were putting on their own clothes, opening jars, and lifting spoons to their mouths with the "useless" limb. In 2006, Taub recreated his experiment with a source group of over 40 patients. All of the patients overcame a condition that Taub called "nonuse" – rewiring their brains to use a limb that was once thought to be lifeless, impaired, and untreatable.

During the pandemic, most of us didn't have our arms in a sling. But we were all impaired. Remember how every day felt like Blursday? We were masked up and asked up to new levels of restriction and constraint.

Here's the good news: Like Taub's patients, we can use restriction to create new vitality, new possibilities, and new opportunities – if we are willing to do so.

Plasticity – the ability to change – is always available (despite what you might have read in 1913). Taub explained it like this in his defining work, *Technique to Improve Chronic Motor Deficit After Stroke*:

Activity dependent brain plasticity can be harnessed through appropriate behavioral or rehabilitation techniques to produce a clinically meaningful therapeutic effect on chronic motor deficits after neurological damage.

Whew. That's a mouthful. But consider reading it again. Look, I'm not a doctor and this book is not dispensing medical advice, but science is telling us something here. For Taub's patients, *their brains changed*. Brains that were damaged by a stroke found new ways of revitalization, movement, and possibility. That kind of change isn't reserved for test subjects: new pathways are available for all of us. A capacity for change is part of the neurons inside your noggin.

Restraints and impairments can lead to greater use, new abilities, and unforeseen discoveries – when we realize that what confined us, reminds us. It does not define us.

Building a blueprint requires some creativity, not responding to stress scares, restrictions, and recent constraints. As we embrace safety, we must embrace our plasticity – our ability to change – and shape a new game. That intention starts by accessing your values.

Remember, how you see your values demonstrated in everyday life can change. And your values can change, too! That doesn't mean you've forgotten what matters; maybe you've found something new to value! That shift could mean you found a new job, left a bad relationship, or converted to Buddhism. Change happens!

That's why exploring how you see your values demonstrated daily can be a powerful path to a new kind of possibility.

Are you willing to change with the times, or do you cling to the past? That's a question I've had to ask myself on more than one occasion. Guess what answer points towards a new expression of my values? Guess which choice gives me new latitude in every aspect of my career and my relationships?

It's easy to think that our potential comes from our past. But that's never true. The past doesn't determine the future. In fact, when we expect our future to be determined by our past, we limit ourselves. We don't step into our potential.

In my past, I've had relationships that didn't work. Bosses I didn't want to work for. A health crisis I didn't ask for, years before pandemic. Does that mean I was broken, weak, foolish, or a failure at the game of life?

I assure you I was doing the best I could with the values I had at that moment. Just like I am now. Just like you are, too. We're all doing the best we can with what we perceive.

When we don't know what to do, it's easy to step into our prior behavior. But yesterday's patterns aren't going to produce tomorrow's results. As Maya Angelou said, "When you know better, you do better."

Do you want to build the future from inside the pandemic – or are you ready to move yourself (and your organization) into a new game?

If you're still reading, I know your answer. So let me ask you two more questions:

- Will you commit to a shared value, with me?
- Will you commit to valuing your potential over your past?

Because, if you will, we can build a blueprint to help you to get there. And, by extension, help your company to grow. The path to growth begins when you elevate the potential of all employees – even the ones you haven't hired yet. Remember, the Stress-Free Experiment asks you to recognize and record how you see evidence of your values in your everyday activities.

If your past doesn't create your future, what does? Think about it. The answer is: the present. Right now is what creates what's next. No matter what you've done in the past, you can choose something different, right now. Here, let me prove it to you: think of a flying pink elephant. With green wings. Wearing a shiny silver tiara. Did you do it?

Have you ever thought of anything like that before? If you said, "Yes, all the time," please be sure to sit next to me at my next dinner party. Because now I'm made of questions.

Perhaps you are capable of thinking of things you've never considered. And playing a new kind of game.

Maybe you're wondering how to change the game for your team, or your organization. Perhaps you were hoping that a blueprint would take shape for your company, your university, your entire sales channel? It already is. We build a world-class blueprint for an organization the same way we build a world-class organization: from the inside out.

You know from visualizing that elephant that you can imagine new possibilities. New ideas are always available; there's no shelf life or statute of limitations on creative solutions. That's true for people. And that's true for entire organizations.

Let's unmask that infinite resource, right now.

You don't always have to eat chocolate ice cream, fight with your mom, or have a drink after dinner. You don't have to always invest millions of dollars in trade shows, limit your investments in the technology sector, or build an organization that's only working when it's working in the office. Culture can change. And if there's one thing the pandemic has taught us: change begins with you.

You can always create an intervention of your own. On a personal level. On a professional level. On every level.

Ready to make some new choices?

OK. I'd like to get that in writing. Seems that a personal intervention is required.

Pick up your pen – the one that Fitch gave you – and start writing about what matters most to you. If you're really committed to personal and professional growth, that says something about your values. Write down the new choices you need, right now, as soon as you're ready.

And then, let's go swimming.

Chapter 4.
Progressive Tolerance

"Yesterday I was clever, so I wanted to change the world. Today I am wise, so I am changing myself."

—Rumi

Remember when you were a kid and you couldn't wait to go swimming? The hint of summer was barely in the air, but you knew it was time to go to the pool! When I was a kid I would jump into water no matter how cold it was, splashing around and having a blast. But, as adults, we don't dive in – we take a few baby steps and we say, "Ooh! That doesn't feel so good!" That fun time in the pool starts with miniature icicles clinging to the edge of your bathing suit!

It takes time to adjust. Takes time to build up a tolerance. Then once we're used to the cold water (which really isn't all that cold; it's just different from the air temperature), the icicles disappear and we forget that we were once shivering. Until we get out of the water! Then we realize – hey, why am I cold again? The funny thing is: the temperature of the water doesn't change. It's our tolerance for the water that does.

When I think back on my own personal health crisis, I did not get super ill super quick. I didn't go straight from a little bit of light fatigue and gaining a couple of pounds to lying on my closet floor crying because I was watching my hair fall out. No, that didn't happen overnight.

What happened was that I slowly tolerated a set of symptoms over time. Those symptoms started to compound. I did everything I could imagine to try and fight back against this mysterious disease. I didn't see how dangerous everything was, at first. I was too busy looking the other way, and building up a tolerance.

I told myself a story. It began with a mythical chapter called, "It's Just a Few Pounds," followed by Chapter 2, "You Just Need a Nap." The plot thickened (and so did I) until it was much more than a nap that I needed.

Same thing with toxic relationships. When things go south with a toxic boss, significant other, or friend, it rarely goes from positive to poison in a single moment. There are always a series of small events and choices along the way that lead us to that place – the place where we stop and say, "How did we get here?"

If you've been there, you know exactly the place I'm talking about. It's the place where the game is playing you. Where somehow you've put yourself in the penalty box, instead of heading towards your values.

There's a name for putting up with stuff that doesn't serve us. It's called progressive tolerance.

Think about getting into that cold pool water: your body is giving you an immediate reaction that says, "You don't really want this!" But a little bit of progressive tolerance, and we push through it, and next thing you know you are swimming along. All is right with the world. Because a little bit of progressive tolerance isn't necessarily a bad thing! As long as you are aware that what you are tolerating is helping you to get to some sort of payoff, desired outcome, or positive result, you are making progress. When tolerance is a choice you are making, with awareness, you might just be moving from sacrifice to reward.

But what about the time when your boss makes yet another really horrible comment, and you instinctively ignore it? Then he steals your idea (taking credit for it himself) and slaps you with a horrible performance review. (Yep, I've been there.) You put up with it, because you don't know what else to do. You feel like you have no other choice. But how does that kind of tolerance help anybody?

Collectively, you look at the behavior and you know it doesn't feel right. You fall into a pattern of "just one more" syndrome. Just one more hour to work on a presentation. That doesn't feel so bad, right? But then you start doing "just one more" three nights a week. Then five. Suddenly, you're feeling off-kilter and burnt out. You know something's not exactly right. But maybe, just maybe, plowing through a few hours on a Saturday will make it better. Except you know how this story ends.

You know the price of progressive tolerance.

I'm not saying you shouldn't work hard. We all have to put in extra time, from time to time. But when we are making sacrifices until we are numb, choices go away. Options are replaced with excuses. Quietly, we force ourselves to adjust to something outside of our natural instincts.

Something outside of our values.

Years ago, I was having symptoms of fatigue and uncontrollable weight gain. The weirdness inside of me was increasing and getting worse, while doctors tried to sort out the cause. My friends, and maybe even my coworkers, realized how sick I was. They saw what I couldn't, because I was suffering from a case of progressive tolerance. I adjusted to my circumstances – just shifting a little bit at a time, so new and stronger symptoms didn't feel that dramatic to me.

It's hard to ignore the "just one more" syndrome when you're suffering from progressive tolerance. Have you been there?

When we're making the choice for progressive tolerance, we don't realize that we're making a choice. If you don't realize you're making a choice, then you're having choices made for you. Does that look like a game-winning strategy?

What is it that we are tolerating, right now? This isn't a book about social injustice or racial insensitivity, but maybe it should be. I don't know about your blueprint for the future of work, but if it doesn't include inclusion and diversity, it's not going to work. What has progressive tolerance brought us, here in the United States? And elsewhere in the world?

If we're going to heal and reveal who we really aspire to be, we need to be better.

Let me speak from my own personal experience, as a woman: Inside any big company, everyone knows who the "bully" bosses are – the ones who might drop the occasional "little lady" reference or come up with some other misinformed perspective. Some have even worse ideas, and predatory actions to match. Yet the discriminatory behavior has been institutionalized, and it continues. Why? Progressive tolerance.

We look the other way in our personal lives as well. Don't believe me? Just read the headlines – any headlines – and see how injustice and inequality are condoned, tolerated, and perpetuated. How much longer do you want to wait to turn the corner on outdated ideas? Designing the future of work requires us to be better.

"Oh, it's not that bad," I can hear you say. "This is what I deserve. I can't expect or ask for more. That's how it goes. This is what I am worth."

These are the words of the devil I know.

But you know what? I learned not to be bedeviled by the voice inside my head. How about you?

CHARACTERISTICS OF PROGRESSIVE TOLERANCE

- Tolerating experiences that are out of alignment with our values.
- Saying, "It's not that bad."
- Saying, "Maybe it will go away," or "This situation will fix itself."
- A mindset that says, "I have no choices. I have limits. I am trapped." Or perhaps, "It's not mine to fix," or "You can't fight city hall." Look for signs of resignation.
- Looking the other way.
- A pattern of repeated fear. Shame. Regrets. A lost opportunity that you just can't seem to embrace, even when it shows up more than once.

Examples of progressive tolerance: Knowing that this is not where you want to be or how you want to feel, your friends/co-workers are telling you that something is

(Continued)

amiss but you keep ignoring it, you see suffering and say/ do nothing (especially if you are the one feeling the pain), you experience pain with no gain (others benefit from your sacrifice). You become numb, unaware of choices and options.

When you do a guided meditation, you spend some time getting very quiet and very still. And as you're taking some deep, cleansing breaths, you're ideally taking yourself to a very calm and centered place. When any kind of thoughts show up – no matter what they are – your job is just to let them pass by. At the end of the guided meditation, somebody rings a bell. That bell brings you back into your present awareness, into the present moment, back into your body, back fully into yourself.

A bell is ringing for all of us, right now. Can you hear that?

It's a ringing that returns us to who we were meant to be. To step into our better selves. To be fully present, right here and right now. Not bound to the lies of the past. No longer tolerating the things that are quietly robbing us of our identity, our creativity, our passion.

We find that new choices are waiting to be discovered. With a thought, we can access a new kind of future – for our careers, our relationships, and our organizations.

We need to heal. We need to play a new kind of game.

We need to move from progressive tolerance to *progressive consciousness*.

PROGRESSIVE CONSCIOUSNESS IS THE PATH TO THE FUTURE OF WORK

Progressive consciousness is what makes us aware of our surroundings and our situations. Progressive consciousness allows us to see that we are making a choice (to get into that swimming pool, for example). Through progressive consciousness, we also see what we are tolerating. We see what needs to change. Progressive consciousness is what allows us to hear that bell ring – and respond in a new way.

CHARACTERISTICS OF PROGRESSIVE CONSCIOUSNESS

- At its deepest level, consciousness contains truth, beauty, creativity, and love. It is the place of awareness, where we recognize the good inside all of us. Our humanity resides there. Our human consciousness is what separates us from the animals, allowing us to be aware of ourselves and others, so that we can work and live humanely.
- Progressive consciousness bravely asks, "What's not working? Why?"

(Continued)

- Progressive consciousness leads us to speak up, speak out, and show up. For ourselves, and for those we see suffering in the loop of progressive tolerance.
- Progressive consciousness prompts the question "Could there be a better way?"
- Progressive consciousness reminds us of self-care: bringing new awareness around the fact that you are worthy, deserving, and abundant. Progress is always possible – and sometimes letting go is the greatest progress you can make.
- Looking squarely at the problem, no matter how big, bad, or systemic it may be, and seeing things in a new (and brave) way. Progressive consciousness points towards the courage inside of all of us.

On the shelf in my living room, there's a shoe box filled with some pictures and mementos. Sometimes I just like to touch some reminders of where I've been, and to see the people I care about (even when I can't do so in person).

I walked over to the shelf, picked up the box, and pulled out a thick stack of take-out menus. I started to laugh, because I remember my friend Rodney had brought them to me in March of 2020: "Just in case this pandemic thing goes on a little long," he joked, "I don't want you to starve." (As a trained chef whose last name means "Let's eat" in Italian, that's never going to be a problem for me!)

I was looking at the eclectic menus from all over town when I felt something strange inside the paper. A plastic piece about the size of a playing card fell onto the carpet. I reached down to pick it up. I was holding a thin white laminated photograph.

"Super Bowl XLVI" was written in bold colorful letters across the top. The picture was from 2012, the year that Indianapolis hosted the Super Bowl. When I was working the game, this was my badge. My identifier. My identity.

There I was: wearing my chef's whites.

I stared at the picture.

I began to cry.

The woman in the picture was forcing a smile. The puffy gray eyes poked out from underneath the chef's hat, framed by frizzy hair that looked like it had been through some kind of electroshock therapy. My throat and shoulders were thick with the signs of the mysterious disease I couldn't shake, revealing the early signs of what I thought was a tumor on my neck. The discomfort of the white chef's coat came rushing back to me in an instant.

I could still remember the smells of the gigantic Super Bowl–sized kitchen, inside of Lucas Oil Stadium, where we were cooking for the VIP reception. As I was setting up my booth – which was called "Say Cheese," if you can believe it – Lenny Kravitz was warming up onstage. In case you are wondering, no, he was not "Gonna Go My Way." But there I was, an "American Woman," and he was 10 feet away from me.

Rockstars on my right and fantastic dishes on my left, while I was stuck in the middle trying to "Say Cheese." Battling a mysterious disease. Wishing that I could be free.

I remembered how good it all smelled, and how bad I felt.

Tears. Again.

I felt so sorry for the woman on that badge. She was me. The me that was.

How did I let myself become this person? How did I let so many things compound, how did I progressively tolerate so many circumstances to get to that point, to become this sad and pained shell of myself? I remember Lenny Kravitz, rehearsing the chorus of "It Ain't Over Till It's Over." I took a deep breath.

A new thought brought me out of the memory. A thought about progressive consciousness.

With a thought, I shifted my understanding. Progressive consciousness reminded me of who I am. I accessed some gratitude: I realized how grateful I am that I am not who I once was. Like you, I am who I am because of my past, and also in spite of it. What's past has passed. The picture is a reminder, not an identifier. Not anymore.

I am here, again, right now. I put the past back into its box. I realized how futile it was to punish myself for the past, or to relive yesterday's pain. Because I know that a new blueprint is possible.

Because I created a new blueprint for myself: a journey of personal healing that continues to this day. I am living my story – a blueprint built on second chances, discovered inside of progressive consciousness. Because we can always begin again.

What's your health issue, or relationship issue, or work issue, that's dragging you down? What's that challenge that's keeping your company from conquering the marketplace?

You made choices that were the best you could do at the time. Isn't that true? Maybe you hurt someone along the way.

Maybe you hurt yourself. Maybe you got sick – you didn't ask for that! Nobody ever does.

Maybe it's time to make amends – starting with yourself.

1. Can you find a way to forgive yourself?
2. Can you put the painful picture of the past back into the shoe box – or into the trash – and move on?
3. You have permission to choose again. That permission doesn't come from me, or your mom, or even some higher power. Permission comes from inside of you. From seeing that the past doesn't control your potential, and it never will.
4. What permission do you need to access, right now? Where's the creativity you need, to find a new way forward?

Sometimes, in a big game, there's a flag on the play. Sometimes you sit in the penalty box. Sometimes there's a "Day of Reckoning" and your snot-nosed little brother cruises right past you in the Game of Life® and you are so angry about it that you wait a few decades and drop that truth-bomb into your book. Sometimes you get four fouls in the final minutes of the game, and you wonder if you're going to sit on the bench. The performance review isn't what you wanted, the bank loan didn't go through, the investors dropped out at the last minute. What do you do now? What's going to help you move forward – and win?

Penalties happen. Mistakes happen. We make choices that seem smart but the referee sees it another way. It's never a question of "How did I let it get that bad?" No, the game isn't the place for introspection – it's the place for execution. Games are for playing. What will you do when you get back on the ice, or on the field, or in the thick of whatever game you want to play?

We need you back in the game, now. Can you hear that? You. Your organization needs you. We need your brilliance and your genius, in the thick of it, creating the future (not reliving the past). In fact, the first step in creating organizational health – and organizational growth – is progressive consciousness. Without your awareness of your values, and your choices, your organization isn't going to get everything you've got. And all the meetings in the world about culture, mission statements, and five-year-plans are going to be met with frustration and misunderstanding. Progressive consciousness is the answer, and the fuel for the journey ahead.

Replaying the last quarter in your mind is only going to create stress. Recreating a life around your values is going to create change.

Leave progressive tolerance behind. Make a new choice. Change the way you play the game. Build the future on progressive consciousness – and let's make real progress together. Here's an exercise to help you to do just that.

Game Changers.

There's something you're tolerating right now, and it's not just a cold swimming pool. Let's dive in on some new ideas – are you ready? Write down the things that you are tolerating, and why. Bring progressive consciousness into play. Not everything that's tolerated is negative, but progressive tolerance can lead to negative consequences if left unchecked. Consider where your tolerance is leading you. What's the price of change? And what's the price you're paying, right now, for ignoring the things that are dragging you down?

- What is it that you might like to change about your circumstances, your company culture, your surroundings?
- Stay open as you create this list. Don't talk yourself out of something. Don't say, "Oh, that's impossible" "Oh, I could never change that" "They (whoever they are) will never listen to me," and then leave it off the list.
- This experiment is for you to explore possibilities – not cut them off before you write them down!
- Finally, what needs to be done to turn progressive consciousness into action?

(Continued)

Writing is a creative exercise – and you are creating your future! Don't worry about your grammar or formatting or any of that stuff. Expand on the Stress-Free Experiment: see the areas where your values maybe aren't coming into play, but you'd like them to! If you're wondering if you should write something down, I offer you my Mangia Mantra as a suggestion: "Why not?" That two-word mantra helped me to write two books during the pandemic, and it continues to help me find new possibilities to this very moment!

Make room for possibilities, not impossibilities. Don't let your progressive tolerance cut you off from what could be! Make a list for yourself. Build one for your organization. Have your team complete the exercise. What is it that your organization is tolerating? What's the obstacle to change that's based on misplaced expectations, past experience, or present misunderstandings? Get those ideas out of your head and onto the page – and you are creating your own *Success from Anywhere* blueprint!

THE SUCCESS FROM ANYWHERE BLUEPRINT

What I'm Tolerating and Why	Hopes, Expectations, and Misunderstandings	What Needs to Be Done – "Why not?"

Chapter 5.

Into the Expanse

"Find the place inside yourself where nothing is impossible."

—Deepak Chopra

"Helping others is the way we help ourselves."

—Oprah Winfrey

I felt trapped.

The room wasn't dark but it needed to be brighter. The light switch was on the other side of the room but I couldn't reach it. Too many people. Too many pieces of furniture. On the ceiling: no light fixture. What kind of cruel trickery was this: a light switch but no lights? I needed to get out of here.

If only I could turn on the light, I thought to myself. Just turn on the light, somebody, please. My breathing was shallow. Quick. Unproductive. What was that technique for regaining my breath? I knew I knew it but I didn't know how to get to it. Just like that light switch. Just like that door.

The door was on the other side of the room. Maybe it was 10 feet away, but it felt like it was in another country. Between me and the door: 11 strangers. 10 chairs. Four tables. And a tour guide. A closed locked door was behind me.

Brown, gold, and copper-colored rocks of various shapes jutted out from the thick concrete walls, as if the outside was trying to come in. We 12 disciples navigated around a concoction of four rectangular tables, polished wood glistening even in the low light. The rectangles met at four points to form a square. At the center of the square, a lonely potted tree, barely three feet in height, winked at all of us. Somehow the pot was sunken into the rectangle, a mysterious patch of dirt hiding the roots that fostered the tiny tree. That plant was just like me. Neither one of us belonged here.

"Get it together!" I said to myself. My breath was heaving, like I was on the 23rd mile of a marathon. The crowd shuffled in a clump of humanity – where were they going? The 10 chairs surrounding the wooden tables, like guardians protecting the transplanted tree, were an orange-red hue. I had never seen chairs like these before. The chair backs were hexagons – stop signs – on top of thin golden supports. They looked like sculptures more than chairs, floating on shining legs. Why were the chairs shaped like stop signs? And why were there so many people in this room? Breathe. Stop. Breathe. Stop.

The door opened, and people began filtering into a new room. Freedom? Far from it. That's not how panic attacks work.

"I can't fit through that door," I told myself, even though people much taller than me were walking through it. "I'm too tall!" my inner voice screamed at me, and that thought played on a loop inside my head. I am almost never the tallest person in the room. This room was no exception. But I was certain that I couldn't leave, because I was too tall. "Calm down," I tried to tell myself. "You're being unrealistic. Get a hold of yourself!" One long slow breath in should do the trick.

Inside of that breath, fear gripped me. Like a huge fist from beneath my rib cage, I felt as if I had been hit from the inside. Four sharp breaths burst out of me. I tried to inhale but my airway wasn't really up for it. Were my lungs shrinking? I leaned down and braced myself on one of the stop sign chairs. Thankfully, the hexagon stopped me from hitting the ground.

That's when I felt it.

A hand on my elbow, and another on my shoulder. "Are you OK?" The touch helped me to steady myself and stand upright.

Tetia, the tour guide, was supporting me. Steadying me. I could see her name badge, thank god – so I wasn't going to black out.

"It's OK," she said, leading me slowly towards the door. "What you are feeling is totally normal." The doorway came closer. I realized I was not a human giant, but actually just myself once again – easily able to fit through the door.

Tetia's voice and words were calming – she talked as we walked. "See, that's exactly what Frank Lloyd Wright wanted people to feel in this room – a sense of restriction, and contraction, so that the transition would be even more dramatic." What transition, I wondered?

Taliesin West was Frank Lloyd Wright's home, workroom, studio, and classroom. In many ways, he was a work-from-home pioneer. From its creation in 1937 until his death in 1959, this structure and the complex of buildings served as the centerpiece of his life's work. Today, this mid-century marvel is the headquarters of the Frank Lloyd Wright Foundation. And on this day, this pre-COVID day, I was taking a tour of the famous facility.

With one tiny step, Tetia led me into the most expansive room I have ever seen. Not the largest, by any stretch, but the most expansive. It was as if the sky had come inside, invited by floor-to-ceiling windows, with a high cantilevered roof that made it seem as if the entire room was floating. The moment we stepped through the door, the light rushed into my eyes and the air returned to my lungs.

Tetia led me to a nearby chair made of wood and brown leather.

"The great artists create emotion in everything they do," Tetia was saying, looking me right in the eye. Before the tour, we had been talking about the architecture of England. Tetia smiled as she said, "Do you think Christopher Wren could have made you feel something like that?"

I laughed, and in my hyperventilated state, my laughter rang out across the main room of Taliesin West. The entire tour turned to look at the panicked blonde woman who was testing her echo-location capabilities. To the untrained eye, it probably looked like I was experiencing a hysterical laughing fit. A joke about England's most famous architect wasn't particularly hilarious, but my breathing made it seem like it was the funniest thing I had ever heard. Tetia smiled and continued in a reassuring voice, "Let's get you back to the group, so you can rejoin the others."

Inside the anteroom, where the tour began, Wright wanted the low sweeping lines of the roof to inspire a feeling that would make the open door seem like an invitation to a brave new world. And what a world it was.

Triangular windows let in the full brightness of the Arizona sun, as the desert rocks and plants were visible through a wall of windows, built in the shape of a lightning bolt (if you can believe it) – an engineering marvel that stretched across the entire left side of the room. Clerestory windows, matched to the triangular roof shape, marked the opposite edge of the room – nearly 60 feet away from where I sat. I walked forward into the floating room.

Claustrophobia has always been a battle for me, made worse by darkness (for some reason). Wright's design achieved its exact intention, and triggered a strong reaction in me – that was the panic attack, brought on by my claustrophobia. This episode was followed by an equally strong reaction in the other direction: no less amazing was the freedom I was now experiencing, inside of this brightly lit space. The contrast from where I had just been was nearly inexplicable.

I stood and turned to Tetia. We walked forward into the great room, and the rest of the tour followed us. "Thank you so much," I explained to her. "I don't know what came over me."

She nodded and smiled. Because she did know. She knew exactly what had come over me.

On some level, she had felt it herself. Not with the same reaction, perhaps, but she knew where I was coming from. She had been there.

She knew that the desert masonry and wooden forms were designed to encapsulate the feelings built into the blueprint by the greatest American architect of all time.

"Come on," she said, "Let's go take a look at the dining room." There, a tilted ceiling blocked the sun from entering the westward-facing windows. The alignment with nature was astonishing, allowing the perfect amount of natural light to take in the interior surroundings, capitalizing on a low-hung design that conquered the heat of the Arizona desert. Wright truly worked in concert with his environment, Tetia explained.

She quoted him: "'No house should ever be on a hill or on anything. It should be of the hill. Belonging to it. Hill and house should live together, each the happier for the other.'"

I felt a renewed sense of belonging myself. I was inside a new space, both literally and figuratively. Now I could appreciate the forms and structures with a new perspective – experiencing that space as something greater than the sum of its parts.

Here's what Tetia the tour guide taught me, in our little exchange:

1. **She heard me, without judgment:** She didn't say, "Wow, there are 11 other people here and none of them are having this reaction. What's wrong with you?" She met me where I was, supporting me in a way that was inclusive and accepting. She didn't offer me a pamphlet on claustrophobia or suggest a 12-week training program; she moved quickly and simply to make sure I was unstuck. My reaction to the feeling of restriction and confinement was OK with her. From there, it helped me to find my way back to being OK too.

2. **She took time to concentrate on me:** Even though there were nearly a dozen other people on the tour, she stopped to make sure that I was alright. She didn't get tactical. ("Here's how to control your breathing. Follow this six-step process in the midst of your unbridled panic.") She stepped back, and took a look at the big picture: "It's only natural to feel what you are feeling," she said. That dose of humanity was more powerful than any strategic guidance. Do you know why?

3. **She offered understanding:** Tetia showed empathy. She knew what I was going through. She shared an understanding that helped me get through it. She understood my

reaction and accepted it as normal, natural, and nothing out of the ordinary.

What can we learn from this tiny episode about handling a crisis, working through fear, and moving through a new doorway? What would happen if we applied Tetia's blueprint to our organizations? In a crisis, compassion is where rebuilding begins.

The tour continued, revealing the furniture and furnishings that Wright and his students had cultivated across his final 22 years. He continually tinkered with Taliesin West, his visions and expectations carried out by his loyal and trusting students. Each winter, Wright and his acolytes would depart the snowy confines of the original Taliesin, in Wisconsin, and come to his desert retreat.

I watched and listened as Tetia explained his meticulous attention to detail, and the deliberate regard for the desert, inside this architectural love letter to Arizona. We entered a cabaret theater. Built with six sides, like the chairs I had seen before, the theater boasted near-perfect acoustics.

From the stage, in a normal speaking voice that carried to every nook and cranny inside the room with ease, Tetia explained how architecture and our surroundings can affect us. While Wright took inspiration from the desert, he took liberties to make sure that each space reflected its purpose.

Inside that small anteroom, I was deeply affected by his artistry, his craft. "The mother of art is architecture," Wright said, "Without an architecture of our own we have no soul of our own civilization."

Brilliant architects design based on how they want an experience to feel and function. What would happen if we adopted

Wright's principles into the world of work? Isn't it true that how you feel impacts how you work? Isn't it true that cultivating a feeling of innovation, for example, is the first step in finding new ideas? Consider how you want your employees to feel, as you remember that our inner world leads us to outward results.

Feeling Fuels the Function

My surroundings in that anteroom – the surroundings he architected – gave me the feeling that the room was shrinking. "Form follows function; that has been misunderstood. Form and function should be one, joined in a spiritual union." That spiritual union told me exit was impossible, the ceiling was closing in on me, and there was no way I could make it through to the other side.

That's how panic attacks work. They operate on a lie of the mind. "The thing always happens that you really believe in; and the belief in a thing makes it happen." Another piece of wisdom from Wright. Tetia shared his words with all of us as the tour continued.

The pandemic left many of us feeling like there was a faraway door that we might never reach. The impossible looked like a place and a time where we could move with freedom, where restrictions were removed.

Many of us have developed our own kind of panic attacks, from inside the worldwide pandemic. Perhaps it's time to unmask those fears for what they are, and move towards that impossible doorway with a renewed sense of possibility?

As a leader, how are you recognizing and acknowledging what you and your team have been through?

According to *Forbes*, nearly 60% of leaders reported that they feel used up at the end of the workday – a strong indicator of burnout (http://bit.ly/km-forbes-burnout). Only 20% of surveyed leaders felt that they were effective at leading virtually. And 86% of high-potential employees report feeling burnt out – an audience that's twice as likely to leave an organization, compared to their peers. The human challenges are many, given recent history. Do you bring the same level of empathy and understanding that Tetia brought to me?

Take time to see that what you are feeling (whatever it is) is perfectly normal. Share that perspective with your team, to the extent you feel comfortable. But first: can you see your experience for yourself? Can you understand that what looks like a simple doorway for one person, or one organization, might appear very different to someone else?

As the saying goes, "You will never regret being kind." The pandemic has been cruel enough. It's time for a deeper understanding. Greater empathy. An empathy that says:

> I hear you. I understand where you are coming from.
> We have all been through a lot. I am here to help guide
> you forward, one step – and one doorway – at a time.

That understanding isn't just a soft skill. It's the hard truth of the future of work.

We need to understand that everyone is processing the pandemic in their own way. As a leader, are you providing compassion and understanding? Are you there for whatever shows up? Are you there, like Tetia, to offer a reassuring hand and a calm perspective? I'm not suggesting you have to have a solution for everyone's situation, but pointing people in the right direction is every leader's job.

For managers and leaders today, notice that you may find hesitation as people move towards the future of work. The hybrid model might seem as simple to you as walking through a doorway, but others might not see it the same way.

For the days after the pandemic, and for the days ahead, inside of a timeless timeframe, we look at what will work not only from anywhere, but anytime as well. Because this pandemic isn't the last business crisis we will face.

Game Changers.

"Don't ask yourself what the world needs; ask yourself what makes you come alive. Because what the world needs is people who have come alive," said Howard Thurman, author, philosopher, and civil rights leader.

Naveed Ahmad is the co-founder and CEO of Flourish, an organization dedicated to human potential – and the never-ending battle against burnout. The mission of Flourish is described simply on their website (http://joinflourish.com): "Unfortunately, in today's society, 'busy = important' and pulling all-nighters is considered a badge of honor. Life is, more often than not, characterized by feeling stressed, overwhelmed, and out of our control. But things don't have to be this way." Do you agree?

I caught up with Naveed for an interview, which was featured in ZDNet (http://bit.ly/km-naveed). Which of these situations describes your own? What is the expansion you need, for the restriction you are feeling right now? Here's what Naveed says:

1. **Sunday Scaries:** By Sunday afternoon at 4 p.m., you begin to dread Monday. And you spend the evening planning so you are ready for your jam-packed week ahead.

2. **Snooze addiction:** The blaring sound of your alarm goes off across the room, and you go to retrieve it. Only to go back to bed. Repeat the cycle 9 minutes later. Then 18 minutes later. Then 27 minutes later.

3. **Increased consumption:** This manifests as the Netflix binge, eating that extra pint of ice cream, increasing consumption of caffeine.

4. **Planning your escape:** You research a cabin to get away to but have no plans of actually making the trip a reality. You fantasize about just getting in the car and driving aimlessly.

(Continued)

5. **Sharp weight changes:** You unexpectedly gain or lose ten pounds in the course of a month.
6. **Counting the minutes:** You look at the clock, and literally count the minutes until the end of a meeting or the day.

Play around with these ideas:

- Adam Grant, Wharton professor and author of *Think Again: The Power of Knowing What You Don't Know,* notes the importance of social systems when battling burnout. Who's your Tetia, when it comes time to decompress and de-stress?
- Write out your burnout battle. Identify the people around you who can help. Is your boss on your list? Maybe he or she should be. And if you are a team leader, write down what you can do to be more like Tetia. Because understanding and empathy aren't just soft skills. Caring leadership is the first step. And it might just be the only way your team is going to move forward into the next room – or the next level. How are you supporting the people who need you most?

Let's Google It

Work happens anywhere, not just in the office. Or is that the home office? Or on the couch? Wherever, whenever. Work is a state of mind as much as it is a physical location. Digital nomads show us how productivity can happen at an RV park, on a secluded beach, or anywhere that the Wi-Fi is strong. The idea of architecting the work environment of the future is about personal choice, more so than corporate edict or office location.

Google had a longstanding tradition before the pandemic: coming into the office was one of the company's few unshakeable rules. The pandemic changed all of that, of course, but now the company wants to architect the return to the office. For years, Google was heralded as an example of exquisite perks and benefits. The inability to provide those extras (think nap pods, vegan chefs, daily massages, and more) was a challenge. Where do you get work perks when you're working at your kitchen table? Google is searching for a new kind of blueprint, right now. Here's what they've discovered so far.

New York Times author Cayce Clifford describes some of the new interior structures under consideration at Google (the company is also a longtime innovator in office planning). Encouraging vaccination (but not mandating it), Google wants to design for the future of work. After input from multiple consultants, the company is experimenting with "Team Pods" – innovative movable work boxes where groups can do what needs to be done (http://bit.ly/km-cayce).

"Each pod is a blank canvas," the *Times* reports, with desks, whiteboards, chairs, and storage units all on wheels, all ready to move and reconfigure. Rearranged in hours or minutes, the Team Pods are built for adaptability. Google is providing equipment for whatever game needs to be played, and letting the employees design what they need, when they need it. Because the future of work is built on choice.

Here are just a few of the things Google is trying out, according to *Protocol* (https://bit.ly/km-protocol1):

- Campfire is a new type of meeting room that intersperses seats with screens to make it feel like virtual attendees have a dedicated space in the room.
- Open-air tents in outdoor spaces allow groups to gather and get work done together. It's like camping, but at the office and less fun.
- Team Pods are basically piles of furniture on wheels that can be easily rearranged to suit the team's needs.
- Inflatable walls can quickly blow up to give a room or a meeting more privacy, and then quickly deflate to open the space back up.
- Office chairs with built-in speakers play white noise to keep distractions to a minimum.
- Hot desks automatically adjust to an employee's settings when they swipe their badge to log in.

You don't have to have the resources of a 100,000-person company in order to see things differently. Creativity is an unlimited natural resource. You can always do things in new ways, regardless of your budget. Like Wright, you can work in concert with your surroundings – you don't have to blow up the mountain or pave the desert in order to create something useful and powerful. Like Tetia, you can find compassion so that the journey continues. You don't need an executive title in order to take ownership of the game you want to play. You can always find new ways to adapt, when adaptability is part of your values.

CREATIVITY
is an unlimited natural resource

The organization of the future operates on:

1. Empathy
2. Ownership
3. Adaptability

That's the new leadership mantra. *Empathy* is your currency. *Ownership* is your contribution. And *adaptability* is crucial for every workspace, marketplace and home office space where work takes place.

The world has expanded. Entering the expanse can be tough – calling up old memories, reminding us of old patterns. No matter where you are, you can choose understanding. That's empathy. You can take ownership of your choices, and make better ones. No matter how claustrophobic you may have felt, you can tap into adaptability. You can instill all three into your expansive blueprint, and when you do, you change the game. You play at a higher level. You see that the pandemic has provided new possibilities, not old restrictions. You are the architect of those possibilities, if you choose to be. Because you can choose how you play the game.

Chapter 6.

Does This Bug You?

"People who are crazy enough to think they can change the world are always the ones who do."
            —Walter Isaacson, author of *Jobs*, the Steve Jobs biography

"It's not enough to be busy. . . . The question is: what are we busy about?"
            —Henry David Thoreau

My college roommate, Kate, was very clever. I could always count on her to come up with new ideas. One night, I arrived at our apartment and found all of my glass cooking bowls upside down on the living room carpet.

Six clear bowls were placed around the room, in between chairs and underneath tables. Was this some kind of craft project? A science experiment? What was wrong with our kitchen cabinets, I wondered? Why would the bowls be upside down on the floor – kinda hard to put cereal in a bowl that's upside down! Kate's door was shut, and it was late. No opportunity to ask her what was behind this new furniture arrangement. Or was this the start of our next dinner party?

I kneeled down to look at one of the glass bowls. Underneath the bowl, bouncing around inside the glass, was a little brown bug. Under a larger bowl nearby, there was an actual grasshopper. Sitting there. Looking at me. From under the bowl.

Each bowl contained a tiny six-legged hostage, trapped in our apartment because we left the windows open. The grasshopper was a refugee from the nearby forest preserve. I grabbed a handy paper plate and slid it underneath the first bowl. Time to free the prisoners.

I lifted the bowl, bug, and plate and shooed the critter out the front door. I repeated the process for every one of our uninvited guests.

The next day, I asked Kate what was going on. She said she needed to find a way to deal with the bug situation.

She put the problem under a glass bowl and went to sleep. The trouble persisted, but it was isolated. Then she chose to look the other way. She went to bed and didn't come out for the rest of the night. Problem solved, right?

Since college, I've seen this story play out inside of companies and organizations around the world. We get remarkably good at being able to identify and isolate a problem. We see that problem through a particular lens (or glass bowl, as the case may be). We see what's wrong. We identify it. We study it. But examination removes us from taking action. Somehow, we hope that someone else is going to deal with what we see as the problem.

Looking at bouncing bugs in a bowl is not a solution. Observation is not an outcome. Isolation isn't the same as action.

OBSERVATION
IS NOT AN OUTCOME

Kate knew she could trust me to take care of the under-bowl issues, and I did. But when it comes to trusting ourselves, we are capable of so much more than just trapping our challenges and waiting for someone else to fix the problem.

In the middle of the game of business, we come together (either online or in person) to look at things "under the bowl." We carefully consider the type of bowl we need, so that we can get a good view of the issues. That way, we can see all of the jumping metaphorical insects we wish to observe. But are we really making progress?

Meetings are often missed opportunities. Don't get me wrong – not all meetings are bad. But I wonder: are you staring at a bug in a bowl, or seeing some real results, when you bring people together? What would happen if you could become more intentional about the way that you design your meetings – what would that do to up your game?

In *Working from Home*, I introduced a four-part question sequence to help evaluate your involvement in any project, meeting, or objective:

1. Does it have to be?
2. Does it have to be me?
3. Does it have to be me, right now?
4. Does it have to be a meeting?

If item 4 resonates with you, then it's time to become more intentional about what makes meetings meaningful. At my desk, I keep a notecard that reminds me not just of what I'm doing, but how I'm being.

After all, I'm a human being, not a human doing. Although on some crazy days it feels like I'm just a whirlwind of activity. You know what I mean? But even at 200 miles per hour, I still have my values – and so do you. We'll learn more about real acceleration in an upcoming chapter, where I share insights from one of the top race car drivers in the world, somebody who literally works at over 200 miles per hour. But first, let's change the game around meetings.

I keep this quote on my desk, the words of Gabrielle Bernstein from her book *Super Attractor*:

> There's no reason for you to play small anymore. The Universe has big plans for you, and it's time for you to claim them.

When I'm "doing" another useless meeting, I find myself looking for meaning. Do you follow me? There's an opportunity cost with every meeting. Opportunity cost means opportunity lost. What if there was a way you could connect, and collaborate, without losing more than you gain?

Game Changers.

Here's how to create **More Facetime in Less Time.** Build this into your blueprint: asynchronous voice and video recordings.

- Think about one person (or group of people) with whom you want more face time. What's the key message you want to convey? What's the desired outcome of your interaction? Then give guidelines to plan your pitch.
- Record the video. View the video. Re-record the video. That's right, One-Take Jake: do it twice. It will always be better the second time around. Especially if you watch it. You have to have the courage to see the cracks!
- Craft a simple message with a link to your video (test your link before you hit send!). Some of my favorite email lines that get people excited are:
  - "To give you time back. . ."

(Continued)

- ▪ "To make it easy to connect without scheduling a meeting. . ."
- ▪ "This two-minute video is an overview of the new idea we've been discussing. . ."
- ▪ "This is not a TikTok video (since I'm a terrible dancer – but, as you know, I'm working on it!)"
- ▪ "This is a meeting minimizer – a quick two-minute video to ask for your feedback/alignment/investment consideration)."
- Great for recognition, thank-you notes, weekly project status updates and weekly team messages. Try it and you'll see!
- Find some examples and further guidance here: http://karenmangia.com/more-facetime

Here's what my audiences are saying in response to my video messages:

- From my pal and *Principles: Life and Work* author Ray Dalio, in reaction to a video about how to make his tools more inclusive and interactive (the short message really made an impression!):

  "Hey, Karen, I love the way you're communicating with me! It's a great way of connecting, and I'm going to pick it up and do more of it. . . . We're just so aligned, and I appreciate your creativity. . . . Here's to the future and thank you!"

- Getting past the gatekeeper: this message comes from a senior executive assistant, tired of saying "No" or "You'll have to wait a month" to people trying to get on her exec's calendar:

  "This is such an awesome idea! I'm going to make video recordings in lieu of scheduling meetings as an option now. Thanks for your continued innovation! Loved the presentation. I hope you're able to get the support you're requesting."

- "Executive Vice President of Emerging Business" sent me this message after I shared a brief video, which detailed an alignment on his goals/priorities/strategies. End result? His agreement to work together on a key initiative:

  "Hi, Karen, I appreciate the creativity of a video message. Well done!"

- I sent a two-minute video to a key executive vice president at a publicly traded tech company. That video resulted in $75K of budget with no meeting. And the approach resonated:

  "Hey Karen, just found a moment to watch your video. Love the idea and the execution of the video message. I think more of these will be in our future. I am supportive of this initiative and can see the benefits of thought leadership in this area. Thanks for leaning into the way we work!"

- I pitched a new pilot idea to a "Senior Vice President of Transformation + Innovation," who said yes to the idea without ever meeting:

  "Hey Karen, Thanks for the message (and video one, love that!). Green light for this idea!"

When it's time to come together, here's how to be more intentional about meetings. You can even change how you participate inside of them, no matter where you are meeting (or where you are in your career). Consider, for every meeting you schedule or attend:

1. **PURPOSE:** What, specifically, is the intended result of the meeting? In order to answer this question, you must shift from descriptive language ("a review of fourth quarter progress, featuring the product development team") to the language of action.

   In *The Art of Gathering*, Priya Parker explains why we meet:

   > We gather to solve problems we can't solve on our own. . . . We gather to make decisions. We gather because we need one another. We gather to honor and acknowledge. We gather to build companies and schools and neighborhoods.

   She says we must commit to a bold, sharp purpose. Are you intentional when it comes to your meetings? Or does progressive tolerance set your agenda? Intentional purpose is focused on action, engagement, and involvement. If your meeting purpose doesn't include interaction and participation at its core, chances are the meeting is really an email. What is the decision that will come from the meeting? What's the homework, next step, or takeaway? How are you going to break people into small discussion groups, so that you can harness the collective power of everyone in the room? If this meeting is an acknowledgment or award of some kind, how will the recognition inspire others (not just the recipients) to do more, be more, achieve more?

My friends, we play small when it comes to meetings. We grab the nearest bowl and put problems (and people) inside it. We don't listen up for feedback. (And yes, I even wrote a book about that subject as well!)

Intentional purpose is the antidote. A bold purpose is wrapped in action, and might even make some people a little uncomfortable. Do you have the courage to hold a meeting outside of your comfort zone?

Ask yourself if that's discomfort, or progress. Do you know what growth feels like? Sometimes taking uncomfortable action around your values isn't as easy as putting a grasshopper under a bowl. But it's a lot more effective.

Wondering whether the meeting should be online or offsite? Confused about whether to find a Zoom room, coffee shop, or a seaside chalet for your meeting? The answers come from your intentional purpose. You've already done the values assessment; now apply the same idea to your meeting and your agenda. The action you want is the purpose – the "where" will flow from there!

Being specific is the key. So many times, we are afraid to be bold, to take large steps, to make meetings meaningful. Stop looking at the glass bowl and calling it a solution. Don't be afraid to have a purpose that pushes – in a gentle and caring way – towards action. Otherwise, why meet at all?

2. **POSSIBILITY:** Reject the template. That's right. Get rid of the old way of doing meetings, if you want to see new results. Yesterday's agenda is not the way to find tomorrow's results. You are designing a new game. What happens if you decide to break a pattern, so that you can solve

a specific challenge? Will people lose their minds, because you've said or done something that they didn't expect? I live for the moments when I say or do something people don't expect – because that's where the creativity is. That's where we find new discoveries. I'm not suggesting you walk around the office trying to scare people, or putting whoopie cushions on your boss's chair. I'm talking about looking into new possibilities – the unexpected discoveries that have led to countless inventions and innovations since time began. If innovation comes from a pattern, then perhaps you should repeat it. But think about that for a second: innovation doesn't come from a pattern; it comes from possibility! Have you ever considered why you are going from one Zoom meeting to another, every day? Or has progressive tolerance made you numb to the fact that this behavior maybe isn't really productive?

Commit to gathering about something

What happens if you decide to have a conversation with your boss to talk about the possibilities, to see what you can discover together? Structure your game around the needs of the business – what would serve your team best? Be careful that you are clear on possibility: you're not trying to dodge a mass of meetings; you are trying to focus on what will help the company most. Priya says, in capital letters, "COMMIT TO GATHERING ABOUT SOMETHING." Is there a meaningful reason for coming together – a reason that expands possibility?

You've probably realized by now that the future of work starts inside of you. Focusing on freedom helps you to play a new kind of game. Sometimes that means challenging beliefs, old norms, and habits. You have the freedom to choose. Find a balance between freedom and feasibility, beginning with your purpose.

THE FUTURE OF WORK
starts inside of you

3. **PICTURE IT:** What is the design that makes the most sense for your meeting? Stafford Beer, the father of cybernetics, said, "The purpose of a system is what it does. There is, after all, no point in claiming that the purpose of a system is to do what it constantly fails to do." Wonder why your meetings don't work? Consider how they are designed. You are the architect of your future. Sure, meetings are required; it's part of everyone's job. But meet me here, and see the possibilities for yourself: what do you visualize as most effective for you? What's the game that's going to inspire you? Are you architecting an expansive view of the future of work? Do you have the courage to share your vision with your

boss, your board of directors, your customers? Challenge beliefs. Find freedom, even inside of the structure of work. That freedom – the freedom to choose – is always available. You might be surprised to find that others are looking for new solutions as well! You don't have to drop every meeting in order to be effective – but being intentional, and deliberate, about how you show up is the key to playing to win.

4. **PERMISSION**: Granted. Are your perceptions or assumptions about meetings correct? You have my permission to test your hypothesis. Start with this question, as you go into the laboratory and begin your experiment: What might I be missing about the purpose of this meeting? What else could this mean, if I could access a new kind of permission (for myself, my team, my organization)? For example, many have believed that the best work happens in a physical office, between the hours of 9 and 5. Well, that story has changed! What's the outdated story you're telling yourself about the value of your next meeting? And how are you underestimating your boss, inside of your story? If you have a business case that explains why changing a meeting (or not participating) is additive for your boss or your company, why wouldn't your boss go for it?

Wait a minute: What do you mean, you haven't given your boss a copy of this book? Time to change that game, *stat*!

If you have a hypothesis that you could find five hours of highly focused work time, delivering 20% more work, why wouldn't that kind of productivity merit a conversation with your boss? Give yourself permission to design a new game!

According to a 2021 FlexJobs survey (http://bit.ly/ km-flexjobssurvey), one of the most valuable aspects of working from home has been the amount of time and money that has been returned to employees. Nearly 40% of employees estimate that they are saving $5,000 a year by working remotely. Why? Because of reduced commutes and travel. And when asked why people enjoy going to virtual meetings, 75% said "not having to travel to the meeting." That's not to say that remote meetings aren't without their challenges. But efficiency is what really matters. The pandemic showed us new possibilities. The future of work isn't about returning to old patterns; it's about finding permission to see things in a new way. What's the fresh start you need, right now, for your next meeting?

5. **PRODUCE IT:** Your commitment is where your intentional purpose comes to life. From intention to impact, you must create follow-through if you want to see new results. For every cynic who says that "purpose isn't practical" or "autonomy is a luxury we can't afford," please stop underestimating yourself. How hard do you want to argue for your limitations? Why not spend that same energy producing new ideas that help expand possibilities? Architecting autonomy begins with the power of choice. Choosing a new way. Choosing to bring intentional purpose to life. Intention without commitment will leave dead bugs on your living room floor. Who wants that? Maybe you'll get a good night's sleep but the problems will still be there in the morning. Exploring values and freedom is important, but

without commitment to new action, new results will never follow. What can you do, right now, to create alignment around your intentional purpose? What action will you take to negotiate new strategies?

Game Changers.

NEGOTIATING THE FUTURE OF WORK: MEANINGFUL MEETINGS

Want to propose a new way of meeting, to your boss or team? Consider:

- **Be the guinea pig:** What if you propose an experiment for the next 30 days, around new ways of meeting, or new ways of participating in meetings? Track your progress – track your experiment – share your results. Talk to your boss, or your team, and share your findings. Are you more productive, or less productive, as a result of your bold ideas? Remember, you don't have to reinvent the wheel inside your little experiment, or cancel every meeting through 2027. Sometimes small changes can create big results. Look for that intentional purpose that opens up possibilities. Take the first step – the first small step. What could it be? Assigning intentional purpose to your work (and your meetings) is an evolution, not a revolution. Break free from progressive tolerance by seeing (and sharing) a new vision for your work success.

- **Make your boss (or your team) the hero:** What happens if your experiment goes well? How awesome would it be if your boss could turn your little experiment into a cultural initiative, where all the senior leaders observe and experience new results? Your ideas are shared, along with the results, because they are too good to be ignored. What might that kind of initiative and visibility mean to your career?

- **Bring progressive consciousness into the game:** Does your boss really know what kinds of obligations and commitments you're carrying right now? Why not? Look, I'm not encouraging you to have a long gripe session about all the things you are juggling. In all fairness, that's why it's called work – and finding your way inside the game is called "your job." I don't mean to sound harsh, but managing commitments is a big part of the game. Progressive consciousness makes us aware of the commitments that serve the organization. Remember, what

(Continued)

matters here is what is going to drive results for the company. Putting bugs in bowls is easy, but not especially productive. What's that action that you can take, from a place of progressive conscious-ness, to find a result that serves your boss, your team, and your entire company? If your solution just makes it easier for you to sleep at night, you might be leaving something for your roommate to clean up. How is that helping your career? Take the entire journey, and discuss solutions (not just observa-tions). Build your business case around actions that serve the team, not just your own personal agenda. What do you think might be the places of objection to your proposal? Notice how your ideas serve the greater good, with actions that can help the team (not just yourself).

- **The playbook is not fixed:** The greatest athletes in the world are the ones who improvise in the middle of the most challenging plays. The game is really on when something doesn't go as planned – yet the greatest players somehow find a way. Can't you do the same, inside the game of business? I'll say it again: the playbook around meetings is not fixed. That means there's an opportunity for you to fix it. What's that look like for you? In the next chapter, I'll share some powerful ideas on what that fix might look like – and how to make change happen.

What we are architecting here is autonomy. Whether hybrid model or working from home, everywhere you go, there you are. Choice is always available. Always.

Choice

is always available

As I've often said, the most dangerous words in business are "That's the way we've always done things."

It's time to choose differently. And it's time to create a team atmosphere that's built on trust. The next chapter will show you how.

Chapter 7.

The Trust Blueprint

"'Trust is built when no one is looking."
—Seth Godin, author and branding genius

Who do you trust?

Sometimes it's hard to trust yourself. Especially after a health crisis. Believe me, I know.

When your body lets you down, where do you turn? You want to believe in yourself, but guess what? Some days are better than others, am I right? That's just the way life works. Expecting every minute of every day to be magic is simply not realistic. I believe in willpower, but I see that there's something more sustainable. Despite our best intentions, we all are capable of putting bugs into bowls, and hiding in our rooms, instead of taking the action that we need. What if there was a way to trust in something more than yourself – something that doesn't change based on moods or circumstances? What would that kind of trust add to your blueprint? To your organization?

"Of all the species on this planet, nothing rivals the complexity inside the human brain," David Eagleman writes in his brilliant book *Livewired*. "The brain is a dynamic system, constantly altering its own circuitry to match the demands of the environment and the capabilities of the body . . . the total number of connections between the neurons in your head is in the hundreds of trillions (around 0.2 quadrillion). Think of it this way: there are twenty times more connections in a cubic millimeter of cortical [brain] tissue than there are human beings on the entire planet."

We are complex organisms – each of us an organization of neurons, notions, and narratives. Eagleman looks at the way that we got here, by examining our internal blueprint. He compares our DNA – the plan for the human system – to the DNA of the Komodo dragon. The heaviest lizards on earth, these modern-day dinosaurs can reach lengths of 10 feet. But can they soar to the same heights that human beings can?

A Komodo dragon from 30,000 years ago, Eagleman says, is basically the same as a Komodo dragon of today. In comparison, the humans of today are much more advanced than the humans of even 100 years ago.

Consider the Flynn Effect. James Flynn, a researcher based in New Zealand, knew that IQ tests are always standardized so that the average score remains 100. So, in theory, a score of 100 in 1921 would indicate someone of similar intelligence to someone who scored a 100 in 2021, right? Wrong.

Collecting test results from World War II soldiers and beyond, Flynn compared results to more modern test subjects from 30 countries. He discovered a startling pattern: his groundbreaking research revealed that our collective IQ is increasing at the rate of three points every 10 years.

Therefore, an average adult who scored 100 on an IQ test today would be considered in the 98th percentile (that would be "super-smart") compared to people from the 1920s.

When Flynn's information was introduced, the American Psychological Association held a conference just to discuss the change in test scores. Were people really getting smarter?

In some ways, yes, and in other ways, no. General knowledge questions (that's the stuff we picked up in school, like what's the difference between a chicken and an egg, for example) barely budged over the course of time. But the performance around abstract theories and concepts skyrocketed. Our ability to understand more shapeless ideas – nuanced topics like "justice," "commitment," and "citizen" – expanded dramatically.

The results are clear: human beings are capable of amazing expansion, even improving our collective IQ, inside of a generation. Beyond the research, how do we know this is true? All you have to do is trust in the design.

"We have tripled our life spans. We compose symphonies, erect skyscrapers, and measure with ever-increasing precision the details of our own brains," Eagleman says.

Unlike humans, Komodo dragons have hard-wired DNA, with simple instructions: "Eat! Mate! Swim! Fight! Sleep!" (and maybe not always in that order). That hard wiring has always been there, and presumably always will be. Eagleman wonders what would happen if a hard-wired Komodo dragon were transplanted from its equatorial habitat to a new home in snowy Canada.

Komodos in Calgary, you say? Lizards in Labrador? Soon after the first snow, there would be no more Komodo dragons in the Great White North. Because these cold-blooded lizards cannot adapt.

Meanwhile, humans have been adapting to various climates and global circumstances (even worldwide pandemics) for millennia.

You and I would do just fine in Alberta, Albania, Alabama, or Argentina. Why is that?

> It's not that we're tougher, more robust or more rug-
> ged than other creatures: along these measures, we
> lose to almost every other animal. Instead, it's that we
> drop into the world with a brain that's largely incom-
> plete . . . For humans at birth, the brain is remarkably
> unfinished, and interaction with the world is necessary
> to complete it. Our DNA is not a blueprint, it's merely
> the first domino that kicks off the show.
>
> —David Eagleman

That's right. The only thing hard-wired into our DNA, it seems, is the capacity to learn and adapt to our surroundings. "Our DNA is not a fixed schematic for building an organism," Eagleman writes, contrasting humans with the rest of the animal kingdom. He's explaining how the blueprint is really designed: "Rather, [our uniquely human DNA] sets up a dynamic system that continually rewrites its circuitry to reflect the world around it and optimize efficacy within it."

THE ONLY THING HARD WIRED INTO OUR DNA, IT SEEMS, IS THE CAPACITY TO ADAPT TO OUR SURROUNDINGS

Scientists probing the mysteries of DNA in 1953 were stunned to discover that the building blocks of our humanity are actually much less complicated than originally theorized. Crick and Watson (the scientists behind the double-helix discovery of the building blocks of life) found that human DNA was relatively unsophisticated, because our blueprint was built for experiences, not hard-wired instinct.

Nature is where it all starts, but nurture – the world around us and our experiences within it – shapes us and makes us human. Our DNA is not a fixed blueprint; that's why we have to create it.

WE ARE BUILT TO CHANGE THE GAME
AND OPTIMIZE OUR CAPABILITES INSIDE OF IT

Human beings dynamically and constantly rewrite our circuitry. We are built to change the game and optimize our capabilities inside of it.

We aren't fixed. Nor are we broken. We are more capable than we realize. Adversity makes us stronger, forcing us to find new ways of progress.

Eagleman's book is filled with stories of people who have had something taken away: loss of hearing, loss of sight, loss of a limb, and more. In spite of these losses and limitations, these individuals have gone on to harness the power of the human blueprint – learning how to read, run, speak, and even "hear," using advanced medical technology that turns human skin into an auditory device.

The book isn't a chronicle of superheroes or cyborgs. It's a story of everyday human triumph based on the miraculous (and unfinished) blueprint of the human system. When a blind person passes her fingers over the dots of Braille, the part of her brain that controls eyesight in others (called the "occipital cortex") becomes active, even though her eyes are not. In other words, her brain has rewired itself to find new resources – using itself and its quadrillions of connections to read via fingertips instead of eyeballs. Touch transforms into a new kind of sight, inside the human brain.

We are wired for competing inside the unknown - adaptation is our nature, no matter how hard we fight it.

Our brains replace what was lost with new neural pathways. New possibilities. New capabilities. A patient who has lost her sight fears she will never be able to read again – the change is too much. Yet these everyday heroes achieve the impossible on a daily basis. We all do. Because we all can.

Rewiring is happening as you read these very words.

You know that you are not the same person today as you were yesterday. The ideas on these pages are rewiring your brain for new possibilities. You don't have to "do" anything. You're already building within the blueprint we call humanity.

Progress is built into the system. It's a fundamental and unchanging rule of the game of life.

We are intricately prepared to walk through doorways, wherever they may lead, in a way that no other creature on this planet can. Our human blueprint won't allow us to regrow limbs, like some lizards do. But our adaptability is actually much more complex, and ultimately, much more expansive, as we can all overcome what's missing by rewiring the most complex and powerful supercomputer on the planet: the human brain.

We are built on an incomplete pattern, and it's up to each of us, from babyhood until our final days, to keep completing the journey. To embrace experiences and innovate inside of them. To keep playing the game.

We need feedback and stimulus to make sense of the world around us: as we learn language, discover how to stand on our own two feet, and ultimately, how to stand up for what we believe in.

But sometimes, the unexpected happens. A pandemic. A panic attack. A financial crisis. A new competitor. What then? New tools are needed to help us adapt. To help us to act. To help us to trust the blueprint inside ourselves. But what about trust inside of our organizations?

According to the 2021 Edelman Trust Index (http://bit.ly/km-edelman2021), business has become the most trusted public institution in the world right now. Business, according to the global survey, is seen as both competent and ethical – blazing past NGOs (nongovernmental organizations), media, and government, in terms of public perception. And a whopping 76% of global respondents say, "I trust my employer."

How will you manage your most trusted resource – the trust of your team, your employees, and your vision for the future?

"We all have a trust issue. We all have a gap," David Horsager says. His trademark staccato is ringing out from inside his Minnesota studio, where he stands in front of a large Rhode microphone, suspended from a nearby retractable stand. Horsager is the author of *The Trusted Leader* (Barrett-Kohler, 2021) and the internationally recognized best-seller *The Trust Edge* (Free Press, 2012). I reached out to David to gain his insights into the fundamentals of building and leveraging greater trust.

"One of our studies showed that 70% of conflict is due to a lack of clarity. If there's one thing you want to change, and measure, inside an organization," he says, "start with clarity."

Communication isn't the problem – communication is everywhere. But clear communication? With actionable guidance, authentic listening and valuable feedback? That commodity is in short supply.

Horsager tells me about a schoolteacher who diligently provides empathy and understanding to his students. He is a man of character: an all-around good guy who genuinely cares about student success. He's transparent, honest, available, and accessible. So why, he asks, are the students frustrated?

Zoom school, I'm guessing?

Nope, that's not the reason.

Frustration exists because the teacher is unclear about their assignments. "The kids end every day frustrated. It's a clarity issue, not a character issue."

The intention is there. The communication is there. Clarity is what's rare.

In a crisis, clarity is crucial. Because crises cause us to rapidly gain trust, or lose it as well. Consider 9/11: the first responders in New York City joined with citizens in a concentrated and trusted effort that banded everyone together. People were running in the same direction.

Not so with the pandemic. Trust has been splintered by misinformation, political agendas, pseudo-scientific arguments, and more. The misdirection is multifaceted – and beyond the scope of this book, quite frankly. So where does that leave us, with regard to the future of work? In the midst of the chaos, what's the path forward?

If you want a trusted blueprint that can work from anywhere, transparency is the key.

Horsager says that people often think that trust equals transparency plus vulnerability.

But is that really true? He knows it's not. What about the folks who are so transparent on social media – transparent with their judgments, slanted political views, epic oversharing, and more? I don't trust them for a second, and neither does he – not because their viewpoints don't align with mine. I don't trust relentless communication when somebody's agenda is always showing. Communication isn't what builds trust.

Clear concern for others does.

Transparency is always evaluated on a personal level. "Our data shows that 92% of employees would trust their senior leaders more if they would be more transparent about their mistakes," Horsager says, adjusting his glasses for emphasis as he quotes the Trust Outlook, his annual study. We don't connect around the triumphs. It's great that you were homecoming king, he shares, but nobody connects on that recognition. "Mistakes make us human," he states, with emphasis. And humanity is what creates the future of work.

If you want to be admired, be sure you keep that homecoming photo nearby and remind people of it as often as you can. But if you want to inspire, remind people that you're not always perfect. Your accomplishments are great, but what you do with that recognition is what really matters.

WHAT CAN YOU SAY, AND DO, TO BUILD GREATER TRUST?

So, what can you say, and do, to build greater trust?

"Don't wait to say, 'I'm sorry,'" Horsager says. "You never rebuild trust on the apology. You might open the door to communication, but you don't rebuild trust."

Think of the person that shows up late for the meeting, and says, "I'm sorry." Actually, no you are not. Because you keep on showing up late. You keep on showing that you cannot keep your commitments.

Your "say and do" ratio is out of whack. Because if your say and do ratio isn't one to one, your actions betray your apology. False transparency is still false, and it can't be trusted. Authentic actions are the answer. You must make sure that you honor and keep your commitments.

Keeping commitments defines your character. A character that people can trust. A character that's built on values – including valuing other peoples' time.

Most importantly, you have to be able to trust yourself. "We only trust ourselves when we make and keep our own commitments," Horsager points out, debunking the idea that you just have to "believe in yourself" in order to work miracles.

Most people don't trust themselves because they don't make and keep their own commitments, and it creates a spiral. A lack of commitment in one area can spill over into two, three, or even thirteen more. Horsager knows the value of a singular personal commitment – because that commitment helped him to lose 52 pounds.

When David Horsager was a kid, he grew up in the poorest county in Minnesota. So having soda – what we still call "pop" here in the great state of Indiana – was considered a real treat. "We never got to have the whole can [of soda]," he recalls. His comment brings me back to memories of my own childhood "luxuries." I can relate.

When he became an adult, he treated himself to sugary beverages on the regular. On airplanes. At dinners. In boardrooms. In hotel conference rooms. One soda became three, and so on.

One day, overweight Dave was sitting in his doctor's office. "You know," the doc told him, "most men in America, if they didn't drink their calories, would lose 30 to 50 pounds a year."

A commitment took shape, right then and there.

David Horsager lost 52 pounds, one soda can at a time. He made a commitment to stop drinking his calories. And the commitment paid off. "I'm still not going to drink a calorie," he says, his thin frame showing the results of his simple choice.

Game Changers.

Ready to find some clarity around trust? Consider these questions. Challenge yourself, and challenge your team, to play:

1. What's the biggest promise you can keep?
2. Write out your commitments to yourself. How do those commitments align with your values?
3. What are your commitments to others, right now? What are the consequences of missed commitments?
4. How can you use communication and conversation to help people to understand your commitments?
5. What can you do or say to gain the help of others, so that you can keep your commitments?
6. Where does transparency come into play for you? Do you have the courage to admit your mistakes?
7. What makes people (including you) decide against transparency? Because oversharing and overcommunicating isn't necessarily transparent, it's just busy. How could you choose your words more

carefully, to come straight to the place where your humanity (mistakes, vulnerability, and all) is actually a superpower? How could greater clarity and transparency make your leadership more effective? Pick one area or challenge and start playing the game a new way.

8. Who do you trust the most, and why?

9. Are you someone that people trust? If so, why? And if no: what can you do to make sure your "say and do" ratio improves today?

10. Why don't apologies build trust? What needs to happen, after an apology, to create trust?

Inside a perfectly imperfect and miraculously incomplete blueprint that we all share, we find the ability to adapt. The basis of that adaptation? Trust. Trust in something greater than yourself.

No matter what the pandemic has taken from you, or your organization, new pathways and new wiring are always available.

Consider these long-held beliefs that no longer fit:

- Myth: *This is just how I'm wired.*
  - Truth: you are always rewiring. You can always realign your circuitry. The human nervous system is built on this premise.

- Myth: *Adaptability must be trained.*
  - Truth: You are not a Komodo dragon. Adaptability is hard-wired into the DNA of every human being on planet earth.
- Myth: *Some people are more resilient than others.*
  - Truth: We *all* have the ability to access resilience. Bouncing back is built into the blueprint.

The ability to design and play your own game: it's always available, even when it doesn't look like it is.

Resilience
is who you are

The human blueprint is extraordinary because it's ordinary. Resilience is who you are. The ability to see and seize new possibilities: that's a part of our DNA. You can honor your commitments in a new way – a way that honors yourself, your organization, and your values.

Booker T. Washington said, "Few things can help an individual more than to place responsibility on him, and to let him know that you trust him." (If Mr. Washington is open to some editing, I would add "her" or "their").

Game Changers.

What might you add to your ability to access the change management tool of trust? How are you allowing your team to take ownership and make choices, right now?

1. Do you trust people to make their own decisions around how to move forward, towards the future of work? Identify specific examples to support what you know is true.
2. Are you providing yourself the permission to try new things – to walk through that doorway, and find what's on the other side? Or are familiar choices keeping you stuck in a tiny room, where old patterns are preventing you from playing a new game?
3. What are the chances that you already know what you need to do, and all that's missing is permission to pursue it?
4. How can you place greater responsibility on your team, and push permission into the organization?

(Continued)

> Where are the places where you can provide greater understanding, in order to help people play the game at their very best level?
>
> 5. Who's there to offer a helping hand, and a word of understanding, when you get stuck? Or are you the one that needs to reach out to someone on your team, right now?

An organization that is transparent, vulnerable, and aligned is able to accelerate around trust

An organization that is transparent, vulnerable, and aligned is able to accelerate around trust. When what you say is what you do, and vice versa, you are playing the game at a new level. Because everyone wants to be on that team.

Moving from intention to impact is possible when we see that new choices are available. Making commitments isn't enough. We have to align to our values, accessing autonomy to consciously choose new patterns (not tolerate old ones). Moving towards discovery, not away from it, aligns us with the blueprint of our humanity. We can, and we must, design the future of work with autonomy and a new freedom of choice. A choice to embrace clarity, transparency, and commitment. A choice to build a say/do ratio of one to one, so that conversations become more meaningful. More real. More trusted. Then, when we access help, and help others, we truly play as a team. A team that can walk through any doorway with ease. A team that can work from anywhere.

Chapter 8.

Finding Excellence

"If you are going to achieve excellence in big things, you develop the habit in little matters. Excellence is not an exception; it is a prevailing attitude."

—Colin Powell, former US Secretary of State

How can you know if a restaurant is truly excellent?

Before you say, "Check Yelp," consider a test that points to something more than just a good review.

Here's how to develop a taste for excellence, in a top restaurant: order the soup.

Soup is an easy place to hide things. Soups are made from miscellaneous bits. Leftovers. Extras. Things that can easily be pureed together or blended in with a bouquet of other flavors.

Here's how soup leads to excellence in a restaurant kitchen. First, stick your spoon into the soup. Pull out a bite. What do you see?

"Cut the carrots!" said the man in the middle of the kitchen. "Cut the celery and onions into small dice. All cubes must be the exact same size!" Chef Karl Benko was teaching his ever-curious culinary students, and I was one of them. In the kitchen, Chef Benko was king. His slicked-back hair, bat-wing eyebrows, and salt and pepper goatee formed into what appeared to be a constant scowl. He always looked like something didn't taste quite right. Quite often, he was correct.

Benko made a name for himself in steakhouses. He was the former director of culinary development for Del Frisco's restaurant group, and a past concept chef at Sullivan's Steakhouse. If you've ever been back-of-house in one of these high-dollar, high-quality restaurants, you know the kind of pressure-cooker environment Benko navigated. He oozed that top-chef intensity in every look, every gaze, every word. Because Chef Benko knew where to find excellence. Today, we were looking inside a bowl of soup.

The assignment was called *mise en place*, a French culinary term that simply means "everything in its place." It refers to the time you spend preparing the ingredients for the meal, before the beginning of assembling any dish in a restaurant kitchen.

How hard is it to cut carrots, celery, and onions into a small dice of the exact same size, you ask? I invite you to try it at home. Let me know how long it takes before you start to scream, pull your hair out, and open a bag of pretzels in recognition of your defeat.

But why would you cut vegetables to the exact same size?

When things are cut to the same size, they cook at the same rate. Therefore, you end up with vegetables that are all done evenly, instead of discovering raw onions and mushy carrots in the same bite. But chew on this: precisely cut veggies are also a demonstration of excellence. In some of the finest restaurants, you'll find where chefs spend a lot of their time, energy and effort: perfecting their knife skills so that every single cut is perfectly even.

I pushed my freshly diced vegetables to the edge of the cutting board. Chef Benko stepped up, took one look, and in a single motion lifted my cutting board off the butcher-block countertop and dumped the contents into a giant stockpot – the place where ugly and improperly cut veggies go. (No food is ever wasted in a kitchen. The stockpot is a place where broth is made, after your veggies are not praised.)

I was not happy. I wanted my work to go into the soup, not the backup stockpot!

"Chef," I asked as my eyes grew larger than dinner plates, "why did you do that?"

Benko spoke simply and without malice. "Wasn't excellent." He reached into the gray stockpot with a spoon and pulled out two carrots, one slightly larger than another. Then an onion that was slightly bigger than its three closest cousins. He threw them back into the stockpot where they belonged.

Chef Benko turned to me and shared the words I will never forget. "Do you want to know the mark of excellent training? Do you want to understand a commitment to excellence, in a chef?" The entire kitchen was now looking at us.

Benko's tone was measured, not harsh or angry. He wasn't upset – he was pursuing excellence. The other chefs had stopped chopping, plotting, and puttering. I wiped my hands on my apron.

"How you prepare the prep – that thing you believe no one else will see or notice – is where you find excellence. If that prep work is not excellent, excellence ceases to exist."

He picked up my knife and began cutting carrots as if he were a two-handed assembly line. Each orange dice was exactly the same as the one before it. "Every time I go into a restaurant," he explained, "I order a bowl of soup." His chopping was even, steady, and perfect – the precision craftsmanship of a master. "I stick the spoon in the soup and when I pull it out, I look down." He stopped chopping and looked right at me. "If those vegetables aren't perfectly cut, here's what I see. I see the level of professionalism and lack of excellence in that kitchen. And in that chef."

He handed me the knife as I looked at a pile of perfectly chopped carrots. "Your turn. Try again."

I discovered excellence on my next go-round. No more veggies in the stockpot.

And, to this day, I always order the soup.

Finding excellence has been the lifelong mission of Tom Peters. The author of 20 books, he penned the perennial classic *In Search of Excellence: Lessons from America's Best-Run Companies* in 1982. His latest, *Excellence Now: Extreme Humanism* is yet another story of our times, our hopes, and our aspirations. I asked him about a blueprint for excellent teams – because a great team is critical to whatever game you're creating.

"Put a musician in there," he says. Wait a minute, Tom, I'm not forming a band. I work at a software company. Where was the guru going with this line of reasoning?

Behind his gray hair and black spectacles, a wall of bookshelves provided the omnipresent backdrop for our Zoom conversation. From his study in South Dartmouth, just outside of Boston, Tom discusses why excellence needs musical notes.

"A musician does not look at the world in the same way that a physics graduate from MIT looks at the world." He pauses to reflect. "I would take every team that I have," he shares, "and load it with English majors, philosophy majors, theater majors, musicians." But why?

Peters explains his simple reasoning. On his team, he's looking for *Range*.

That's the 2019 book by David Epstein, with a powerful subtitle: *Why Generalists Triumph in a Specialized World*. The premise is counterintuitive: popular theory says that intense focus and specialization on a particular skill is the best way to master it. Seems like a team of specialists would specialize in success, right? Wrong.

Taking a fresh look at the top performers in the world, from athletes to Nobel Prize winners, Epstein proves that specialization isn't the path to peak performance. A broader range of interests, habits, and techniques is.

In fields where performance is relatively simple, with a low level of unpredictability, specialization can be useful. Consider young Tiger Woods, learning to swing a golf club as a baby and beating his dad by the time he was eight years old. It's the classic story of specialization. Seems to build a case for intense focus, right? Ten thousand hours and all that jazz, right? Epstein shows that an intense focus can be good for simple, repetitive tasks – such as swinging a golf club.

Golf, he says, is a "kind" learning environment. He explains the kind learning environment using the game of golf as an example. Consider what happens when a player drives a golf ball: it either hooks, slices, or goes straight:

> The player observes what happened, attempts to correct the error, tries again, and repeats for years. . . . The learning environment is kind because a learner improves simply by engaging in the activity and trying to do better.

Is your business like a game of golf, where the rules are clear and complete, patterns are repetitive and obvious (like landing in a broad green fairway), and feedback is instantaneous, precise, and accurate?

In a word: no. Golf is the escape, not the metaphor, for the business world. That's right: for everyone who is sick of sports metaphors in business, hear these words. Golf is a terrible metaphor for business. Because the world of business is not a kind learning environment – it's something else entirely.

The world of the knowledge worker is filled with unclear objectives, uncertain rules, and questionable feedback. During the days of the industrial revolution, repeating activities over and over with minor corrections for the business equivalent of a slice, we developed a "kind" recipe for success. Today, unless you are an assembly line worker – or a caddy – golf is not what business looks like anymore.

Today, workers aren't matching a pattern to hit a fairway. We are creating a pattern – and sometimes even finding a brand-new fairway – every day.

Peters and Epstein agree: If you want to play like Tiger, get clever like Fitch.

Business isn't a "kind" learning environment; it's what Epstein calls a "devilishly wicked" one. A devilishly wicked game has uncertain rules, multiple competitors, no established patterns, changing rules . . . you get the idea.

A change in the status quo can rob us of the advantages of experience in a devilishly wicked game. Epstein uses the example of firefighters asked to take on a burning skyscraper. Suddenly, they are deprived of the expertise and intuition gained over years of battling house fires. When the game has changed, the players have to change with it. Or their chances for victory go up in smoke.

Peters is playing a game of excellence, and he's an advocate for new perspectives in the face of relentless change. Diversity in all its forms is the shape of excellence, in the future of work. Diversity of perspectives. Backgrounds. Orientations. Viewpoints.

Specialization is good, but a broad range is better. A flexible combination is the most excellent of all. What else does Peters see, in the *Success from Anywhere* blueprint?

"One of the things I would put right at the top of the list is listening skills." I hear that.

The arbiter of excellence explains, by way of a story:

Consider a salesman from your company. He is speaking with a woman, and the salesman has been instructed to ask a series of questions. When the woman is two sentences deep in her first response, the salesman interrupts her and goes on to the next question. This pattern repeats itself, and the salesman gets to the fifth question. He gives her some spiel of features and benefits, before he pauses and asks, "What do you think about that?"

The woman doesn't open her mouth. Ten seconds pass. Then 20. Then 30 seconds more. The salesman says, politely, "Aren't you going to answer?" And she says, no, I didn't see any reason to waste my time answering because you answer all your own questions anyway.

Funny how checking off the boxes and matching a pattern isn't the pathway to success. In fact, doing everything right without taking time to listen isn't anywhere near excellence. It's the exact opposite.

Success isn't a punch list. The wicked game is filled with nuance and change. Repetition without correction is a fool's game. Without feedback, how can any of us play to win? Applying a pattern was a great idea for Henry Ford's factory. And for your swing on the fourth tee.

In that kind of unpredictable environment, mechanics matter. And that's not to say that some understanding of mechanics isn't vital to the execution of every role. But what Peters is saying is that mechanics are only part of the story – a very small part, when faced with a changing environment that demands innovation, invention, and expert communication.

Here's more wisdom from Tom Peters, as I shared on ZDNet (http://bit.ly/newgoldenrule):

Karen Mangia (KM): How do leaders cope – and perhaps even thrive – as they move forward with their efforts to serve their team members, the communities in which they are embedded, and the planet itself, amidst this uncertainty?

Tom Peters (TP): I started hearing from leaders around the world. They were looking to me for guidance, to find a path forward in these uncertain times. The abundance and the urgency of those inquiries lead me to create what I refer to as the Leadership Seven, [post-]COVID-19 edition:

1. Be kind.
2. Be caring.
3. Be patient.

4. Be forgiving.
5. Be present.
6. Be positive.
7. Walk in the other person's shoes.

KM: You coined the phrase *extreme humanism*. What does that phrase mean, and how can leaders exemplify extreme humanism?

TP: Extreme times call for an extreme response. And what we all need to do right now is to practice being extremely human. We need to practice the courage to show up as our authentic selves. We need to practice the courage that comes with being real – chatty children, barking dogs, and all. Everything and everyone that shows up on our video screens is an opportunity to be extremely human. One of my favorite books is *Kindness in Leadership* [by Gay Haskins, Michael Thomas, and Lalit Hohri; Routledge, 2018]. Practicing kindness as a leader is the best strategy to tap into our humanity and to deepen relationships and trust. Being kind is at the core of being extremely human. Being extremely human is at the core of being a great leader.

KM: That reminds me of your six-word story – the six words you say best summarize your life and the six words that should be the North Star for every leader now.

TP: "Hard is soft. Soft is hard." What I mean by that is "hard" (plans, numbers, spreadsheets, organization charts, process maps) is "soft" (abstract, malleable). "Soft" (people, culture, relationships, world-altering design, commitment to excellence) is hard (enduring). Relationship development epitomizes the "Soft is hard" idea. Hence, what I suggest is that every leader put a formal plan in place to guide your ongoing investment in relationships. What – precisely – is your formal relationship investment strategy (RIS)? What is your RIS for today? For the week? For the month? We commit to strategies when we write them down. I suggest every employee in every organization draft such a plan.

KM: You assert that enterprise excellence is about just two things. What are they?

TP: Enterprise excellence is: 1. People. 2. Service. Excellence equals service. Service to one's teammates, service to one's customers and vendors, service to our communities. In a sense, service to humanity.

KM: You share in your book that you dream of an "excellence revolution" and are frustrated by the lack of progress. What's keeping us stuck, and what's the catalyst for individuals and for organizations to spark an excellence revolution?

TP: I receive lovely feedback about the transformative power of excellence, but have been enormously frustrated by the lack of an "excellence revolution." While any number of leaders have bought into the concept – especially in small- and medium-sized enterprises – unballetic enterprise performance has remained the norm. We're lacking the skillful choreography of excellence as a practice, as an expectation, of every employee enterprise wide.

KM: Each one of us could launch an "excellence revolution" right now, by following your version of the golden rule.

TP: My version of the golden rule – a rule that anyone can follow – is: Always positive. Rarely negative. The research shows that positive reinforcement is 30 times more powerful, in general, than negative reinforcement. And I believe that golden rule is even more true in today's virtual world.

How could you implement Tom's golden rule in your next conversation? What would it mean to your organization to launch and to sustain your own "excellence revolution?"

The requirements for excellence begin with really being able to grasp feedback and apply knowledge in new ways, to navigate through uncertainty. That's the first step in a positive direction.

Tom continued to share his insights with me. "How are you, as a human being, making judgments in a professional way?" he asked. No matter how technical your field, he argues, you are involved in a people business. "In *Humanism*, I wrote about the biotech CEO who says, 'We only hire nice people.'" If you want great results, Peters says, hire for *empathy*. "I don't care how obscure the technical qualifications might be. There are people who have the same technical qualification who aren't jerks."

"My pal Harvey Mackay wrote about how to *Swim with the Sharks*. He tells the story of how his final exam for hiring somebody was to take the candidate to a Minnesota Twins baseball game. The goal was not to find out if someone knew the difference between a balk and a double play, but to see something more important. How did they deal with the popcorn vendor? Did this person wait in line?" Seems to be a scenario that reveals character. And empathy.

What's the approach when you can't go to a Twins game, I wondered. How do you observe and access excellence, one inning at a time?

Excellence, Tom Peters says, can't be taught or trained. It can only be modeled. And he's been modeling it for over 40 years. His remarks reminded me of what Chef Benko showed me in the kitchen. When he spoke to me about precision and excellence, he demonstrated it with every staccato stroke of the knife.

As leadership expert and best-selling author John C. Maxwell said, "A leader is one who knows the way, goes the way, and shows the way."

Accessing excellence is a path we can all access

Turns out, accessing excellence is a path we can all access. Because you – and anyone else on your team – can find success in the next five minutes.

I call it the *five-minute fix*.

Game Changers.

The five-minute fix starts simply: it begins with a pause – a pause where you reflect on how doable a five-minute fix really is. You can do almost anything for just five minutes, right?

So ask yourself the additional questions, while you're taking a moment to pause:

1. What's working, and what's not working, right now?
2. What's the smallest thing I can give myself permission to adjust?
3. What happens if I spend five minutes working on that?

Consider the person who's working at home, still, even though she thought the change was temporary. She's still in the antique dining room chair, working at the kitchen table and progressively tolerating an ongoing backache. The five-minute fix takes five minutes to look up new chairs online, and she discovers how comfortable those gaming chairs are.

In less than five minutes, she's discovered a modern and comfortable adjustable chair. Later that same day, she takes another five minutes and orders the chair.

(Continued)

When it arrives, she unboxes it in five minutes, realizing that the setup is more than a five-minute fix. But the unboxing – and blocking half an hour on her calendar – still takes less than five minutes.

What is the think-big, act-small, five-minute fix you need right now? Could you add that five-minute fix to your values? What would happen if you did? What if you were five minutes closer to excellence? That's a time frame that anyone can handle.

And speaking of time frames: what if there were ways to change your relationship with obligations, and reconsider what time management really means? Our next chapter looks inside of walls, to find ways to break through them. An excellence revolution may be closer than Mr. Peters realizes – that is, if you want to add that revolution to your values and serve at a deeper level.

Are you ready to model a new commitment to excellence?

Chapter 9.
The Slap, the Liar and the Racecar Driver

"Acceptance doesn't mean resignation; it means understanding that something is what it is, and there's got to be a way through it."

—Michael J. Fox, actor and advocate

"Not everything that is faced can be changed. But nothing can be changed until it is faced."

—James Baldwin, novelist and social activist

ACCEPT. ADAPT. ACCELERATE.

These three words have been the subject of countless trainings, keynotes, and conversations for me, helping to provide a simple structure for leading through change. When it comes to playing a new game, these three concepts create a powerful playbook for new possibilities. Nathaniel Branden, the Canadian therapist who pioneered the psychology of self-esteem, said, "The first step toward change is awareness. The second step is acceptance."

Why is acceptance so vital to managing change?

Accepting what is will **open new doorways** to success
Accepting what is will **lead you** to what could be

In her book *Loving What Is*, Byron Katie explains the source of our discontent: our inability to see and accept the reality of life around us. The cause of all suffering – that's right, every discomfort and discontentment and challenge and overwhelm and you name it because you don't like it – comes from one single source. That source? What we are thinking and believing.

Not what we are accepting. Not what we are acknowledging. Not what we are seeing, but how we are processing (and thinking) about the people, places, and things around us.

Byron Katie tells an amazing story that, for me, captures the essence of acceptance. In a live presentation, she asks the crowd, "Imagine that someone comes up here, on stage, and slaps me across the face." The crowd gasps. "What am I going to do?"

What would you do? What action would you take?

Are you already plotting your revenge? Ready to counter-punch? Wishing that you had blocked that slapshot? Wondering if you can run away, grab a baseball bat, or a good hiding place, or what exactly?

Here's what Byron Katie shares:

"I say, 'Thank God that's over.'"

Acceptance. Not revenge. Not defensiveness. Not creating a story about cruelty or the unfairness of getting slapped.

Acceptance. Accepting what is.

Notice that acceptance is not progressive tolerance. Progressive tolerance is standing there and waiting for the second slap, then telling yourself a story about how you deserved that first one, and probably the second one as well – because you can't ask or expect anything more from this cruel world. After all, the self-sabotaging story goes, life is just one slap in the face after another.

But Byron Katie wants to break that pattern. And so do I. As Byron Katie says, "Who would you be without that story?"

The answer, my friend, is someone who stops getting slapped.

I worked for a boss who was undermining my work at every possible turn. The first six months – I'll call it the honeymoon phase – were great. But then things started to take an eerie turn. He would set up meetings with my employees and ask them to work on projects – projects where I had no visibility! So I had no knowledge of what was being asked, or why these "skip-level" meetings were taking place. (Makes it tough to lead and manage your team when you don't know what they are working on, because your boss is making the assignments instead of you. It's the classic definition of "undermining someone's authority" – and this passive-aggressive move was not cool.) My employees would explain that they were stretched too thin. People complained of all these deadlines. I said what every great team leader should never say: "What deadlines? Huh?" Hashtag clueless: I was in the dark. Because someone else – my boss – was writing the rules for the game. And keeping me on the sidelines.

Of course I confronted my boss. "Please give me a heads up on any assignments or tasks you give to my team, so I can help make sure you get what you want." Gotcha, was the reply – no problemo.

A few months go by. Friends start telling me that my boss is not who he seems to be. I observe a conversation with him where he is trash-talking one of his team members, telling me that she is a despicable person with no talent, no skills, and so on. He's really tearing into her performance and personality, with no holds barred. She's terrible at this, horrible at that, incompetent and incapable . . . when that very same person passes us in the hallway. "Oh hi!" he says, changing his personality on a dime. He gives her a big hug and compliments her on her recent projects, without missing a beat.

I. Was. Stunned.

The guy's narrative changes from terrible to terrific in one chilling instant.

That was when I realized I was working for Dr. Jekyll.

And when it came time for my performance review, I met up with Mr. Hyde.

In every area – every area – I received top marks for my contribution: 10 out of 10. Every area except one.

That area was "promotability." And that score? Zero.

The other scores were put together based on 360-degree feedback – colleagues, co-workers, peers, and team members. But one category, promotability, came from a single source. That rating – that big fat zero – came exclusively from my boss.

My friends and colleagues had been telling me to watch out for this guy. "He doesn't have your best interest at heart," one said. Another told me, "He's not who he appears to be, and behind your back he won't hesitate to throw you under the bus, climb in that bus, put it in reverse, and make sure he finishes the job."

A good friend whom I really respect made an unprecedented move: she not only found a new boss, but she moved her entire team into a new reporting structure. She lifted and shifted an entire chunk of the organization – and took her team to greener pastures. Why hadn't I done the same?

The signs of deception and undercutting were everywhere. The message was clear, but I wasn't willing to listen. That hard, slow slap was coming for me. I kept my eyes shut because I didn't want to see what was happening. "Keep your head down" was my mantra, when it should have been, "Keep your eyes wide open."

My response to the deceptions and backstabbing was what it had always been: progressive tolerance. "Things will get better," I told myself. Continuing to execute on my objectives, I ignored the fact that a leopard can't change his spots.

When the zero hit me, in that performance review, it was like a hard slap in the face.

The evaluation was a lie. When it was over, I made a shift.

I dropped my story. I stopped the progressive tolerance and the narrative that enabled my ability to look the other way – or just to keep my eyes shut, hoping things would get better. I opened my eyes and stopped looking in the direction of denial.

I moved from progressive tolerance to acceptance. Which, as Michael J. Fox says, is not resignation. Acceptance allowed me to adapt. To take action, instead of taking whatever was being given to me.

Instead of taking a lie and making it part of my identity, I found my voice.

Before I found acceptance, before I found my voice, I was lost in a story of false hope. My false hope was wrapped inside someone else's narrative of deceit. An undercutting story about my performance and my commitment and my career: the whole experience was beyond the pale.

Hopefully, you can appreciate the desire to see things in a positive light, even with a bad boss – which is where my intentions began. There's nothing wrong with wanting to make the best of a situation, especially a difficult one. But what's the path to truly making the best of a difficult situation? Telling yourself a story, or accepting what is?

As Byron Katie says, I had to take a look at my story. I had to ask myself, "Is that true?" Is it true that things are going to get better when every indication is that they are getting worse? I paused – about the amount of time that it took for someone to pull back their hand and aim it at my head.

The slap was delivered, and it stopped my career in its tracks. It wasn't easy, but I managed to say, "Thank God that's over." And I realized that I could move forward and make a change.

Was it as simple as that – just "making a change"? No, my friend, it was not. Sleepless nights and worrisome days were the price I paid for a story that didn't serve me. A story that made me question my values – and my worth.

Have you been there? Have you been handed a story from somebody else, about who they say you are, and you know it's not true?

You can't work from anywhere when you're living inside a story like that. Because that story won't work for anyone. If you're living a lie that someone else passed on to you, it doesn't matter what culture your company has or whether you are a digital nomad or what your subject matter expertise might be. No matter who you are, or where you are, you can't work inside a lie. Someone else's story isn't going to help you access your truth.

In the course of my work with my bad boss, I had documented a series of events with an email trail that reached from Oregon to Oklahoma. The journey was well-documented in black and white. Of course, I didn't always see the warning signs and the pitfalls and the undercutting and the backstabbing. But my HR department did. Their story was different from mine, and it started with the words "Hostile work environment."

Moving from acceptance to adaptation, I surrounded myself with people who had my back, rather than people who wanted to stab me in the back.

What might have happened if I had said, "Thank God that's over!" sooner? What might have happened if I had put my best energy and effort into creating new choices and moving forward?

Acceptance would have moved me from victim into a position of action. From reactor to actor. Instead of being sidelined by a bad call, I could run a new play. And that's exactly what I did.

I wonder: how long do you want to wait, before you say, "Thank God that's over?" When is the right time to drop that story you've been telling yourself? When do you want to take back the ownership of the game you are creating? And who's there to help you to make that move?

It's amazing what a fresh perspective can reveal, especially a perspective that's outside of the progressive tolerance and stories we make up for ourselves.

In my situation, I adapted to "what is." I found an advocate and an ally inside the culture of the organization. The performance review was reversed. Dr. Jekyll went back to his laboratory. And I moved on, shifting to a team that has been nothing but supportive of my ideas and my contribution.

It bears repeating: acceptance is not resignation. Accepting what is will lead you to what could be. Without acceptance, you're solving imaginary problems while denying real ones, while you wait for your next slap. How can you work from anywhere if you don't see the work that really needs to be done?

New perspectives are possible when you step outside of the story you are telling yourself, and the lies someone else is handing you. Because you don't have to play someone else's game, particularly when their rules have you in the penalty box for a foul you didn't commit – and never would.

So: what shows up on the backside of acceptance?

Understanding. And opportunity.

An opportunity to adapt.

I've shared the importance of adaptability in prior chapters. For our purposes now, I wonder: what needs your acceptance right now? What do you need to see with greater clarity – outside of the story of progressive tolerance you're telling yourself?

And from that place of acceptance, what's the adaptation that makes the most sense for you? How can you step into progressive consciousness, and see what's next from a place of greater clarity?

The pandemic was like a slap in the face, wasn't it? Maybe a slap in the face and a punch in the gut and a karate chop to your kidneys and . . . I could go on, but you get the point. Are you ready to say, "Thank God that's over?" Are you really ready to adapt? Are you ready to take action, and get back to the game you really want to play?

When I find that I'm ready to make some real progress – when I'm interested in moving forward in my life and my career – *acceleration* is on my mind. I want to know the shortest and fastest route to new success. Always. How about you?

I reached out to someone who knows more about acceleration than anyone I know.

James Hinchcliffe has competed in nine Indianapolis 500 races, including a seventh-place finish in 2020. He's been a race car driver, professionally, since 2011. When I caught up with him (and believe me, it wasn't easy), I asked him about working from home when your "home office" goes 235 miles per hour. What's the secret, I wanted to know, behind true acceleration?

Hinchcliffe knows all about the risks associated with moving fast. Coming around turn three at Indianapolis, in a practice session, a freak accident caused his car's front axle to break off at 230 miles per hour. The broken axle pierced the interior of the race car – and the interior of James Hinchcliffe. "I was literally a shish kabob," he says, recalling that fateful day in 2015. Teams of first responders raced onto the track, maneuvering to get Hinch out of the car, into an ambulance, and on to the hospital. The accident nearly killed him.

Ever the fighter, Hinchcliffe bounced back from near-fatal injuries to learn some new moves of his own. Eighteen months after the accident, in 2016, he appeared on *Dancing with the Stars.* Hinch finished first runner-up on the show.

So, is acceleration all about learning new choreography? What's the connection between the track and the dance floor, when your "home office" can cover the length of a football field in less than a second?

Hinch explained how his world works: Indy cars are basically bullets, suspended between four tires, weighing in at just over 1600 pounds. So, for comparison, an Indy car is about half the weight of a 2021 Toyota Camry, and the exact same length. While precise horsepower is a closely guarded secret, these road torpedoes squeeze something close to 700 horsepower out of a typical 2.2-liter Honda engine. Meanwhile, in the grocery store parking lot, the Camry delivers a snappy 206 horsepower, and hits the redline at just over 6600 rpm. These numbers don't mean much to me, but when you compare it to a race car, it starts to make sense. (Check out http://bit.ly/km-indycars for more info.)

The engine inside a race car screams to over 12,000 rpms, propelling the road rocket past 225 mph in a matter of seconds. Taking the Indy car into a turn results in a 2.26 g-force. So a 160-pound guy like Hinch is gonna feel 361 pounds of pressure every single time he turns the car. The midpoint of a turn ratchets it up to 3.1g. That g-force is the equivalent of having a sumo wrestler sitting on your lap while reaching across your face for an extra helping of pasta alfredo. While you try to steer the car.

"The cockpit isn't like any car you've ever driven," Hinch explains, pointing at the interior of car number 29. "The seating position is akin to sitting in a bathtub, with your feet up at the faucet level. You sit very low, with your feet up higher than your derrière." Hinchcliffe, a Canadian, is evidently fluent in French.

"The seat is custom made – and custom molded to the driver. As you can see, there's not a lot of elbow room. So if you're claustrophobic, you're going to struggle inside one of these cars."

I can feel my smile tighten into a thin line, and my brow wrinkles. "Hey, Karen," he asks, noticing the frown that's taken over my face, "you're not claustrophobic, are you?"

Never mind about that. Luckily, you're the driver, not me. Let's just talk about that steering wheel, shall we?

"The steering wheel is the brain of the car," Hinch says, pointing out that the "wheel" is really more like an integrated instrument panel, positioned between two handles. It's not round at all, but flat on both the top and bottom. It's a miniature scoreboard, complete with blinking lights and numerical readouts. The flat "wheel" dominates the driver's field of view, inside the car. The clutch and gears are both on the back of the steering wheel, behind the onboard computers and external buttons that control different settings on the car.

So out there on the track in Indianapolis, with 32 other competitors, where do you place your focus? Where do you look, and concentrate, to make sure you position yourself to win?

"Some guys perform at a high level when they are angry," James tells me. Wait a sec – some focus on their emotions, not their driving?

Hinch shares that those emotions blur his ability to navigate on the track. He puts his feelings in the trunk, while accepting the multiple inputs and competitors as they are. There's no time for managing emotions at 235 miles per hour. He's got to concentrate on the task at hand – not how he feels about it.

Distractions are disaster

The task at hand means holding on to that wheel while wrestling the car into hundreds of turns, receiving headset feedback from your crew, managing to keep ahead of other drivers . . . the myriad of inputs and stimuli is mind-boggling to me. "I focus on my lap time," he reveals. "That's the one thing that I can control, the one thing that I am really pursuing. Am I better on this lap than I was on the last one? Am I maintaining or improving?" Success, inside an Indy car, is all relative.

Maybe that relative equation is also true outside of a blazing road bullet on four wheels. Maybe the way to accelerate in your career is by shifting your focus.

I wonder, dear reader, what's your lap speed right now? What's one thing – one five-minute fix – that could help you to accelerate in your career? Maybe instead of developing a BHAG (Big Hairy Audacious Goal) or working on your SMART goals, or exploring some other clever mantra, it's time to access what really works. Perhaps there's another place to look.

A SIMPLE 1% DAILY IMPROVEMENT
will double your results in 72 days

Remember, a simple 1% daily improvement will more than double your results in 72 days.

The takeaway here is that big goals are nice but making do with what you've got is the only way to accelerate from where you are. Incremental steps can secure your success in a more powerful way than outlandish stretch goals.

The key to massive acceleration isn't chasing the impossible. It's doing the do-able.

DO THE DO-ABLE

What happens if you take what you've got and concentrate on small improvements, just a five-minute fix, instead of trying to conquer the world by next Tuesday?

For me, for a long time, it looked like striving and grinding and pushing and planning were all part of the recipe for success. I had to have my foot on the accelerator at all times.

Hinch sees it another way.

"You only have to be faster than the next fastest guy. You don't have to be the fastest person that's ever driven on that track and in that type of car. You just have to be the best person on that day," Hinch explains.

The game gets good when you are just a little better than you were before. When your acceleration is relative, not necessarily superlative.

Pushing your car too hard is an unnecessary risk, Hinch says. "You can practice all you want but you're always going to find yourself in race situations that you didn't necessarily practice for. And how you react in those moments is absolutely crucial. So, for me, gut feel is the greatest part in all the preparation."

Sounds like a wicked learning environment to me. Hinch agrees.

"Inside the race car, you have to slow down." Hinchcliffe follows his own lead and slows down to look at me. "Here's the deal. You have to go slow to go fast," he says.

Go slow to go fast? I didn't expect to hear that from a race car driver.

So it's not always about pushing yourself to your limits or going as fast as you can. It's about being in time, and being on time, that really matters. Slowing down your thoughts so that you're not filling your brain with distractions. Slowing down so that you can see what is, versus what your mind is making up about the inputs and outputs all around you. From this place, Hinch shares, comes true acceleration. Because you are able to see new possibilities – new ways to propel yourself to the next level.

So many times, what we think is needed is actually working against us. Like Hinch on the racetrack, I've often felt like I needed to ramp it up – and take it out as hard as I could. Faster is better, right? That's what I told myself, as I was racing past the moments that mattered – missing opportunities to truly accelerate because I had my head down and my foot on the gas.

Even when going that fast actually slowed me down – sending me, at one point in my life, into a health spiral that I thought would never end.

Here's what Hinch sees, around acceleration – but you have to slow down to see it:

1. Pushing yourself (and your vehicle) all the time isn't a winning strategy. Ever.
2. Knowing your limits and accepting what is allows you to truly make improvements and go faster, when your mind is clear (not cluttered).
3. Going as hard and as fast as you can increases risk. (Do you need a pit stop? Time to refuel, so you can continue the race?)
4. Incremental improvements are all that's needed to win. Because you've got to slow down to go fast.

I shared with James how I notice how much I need to get out of my own way when I play the piano. When I'm playing a piece of music, the second that I start thinking to myself, "Where am I?" is when I lose track. And when I'm not thinking about "Where am I?" I'm fine. Tuning into the thoughts around my performance is what takes me out of it.

Commenting on the performance inside my head, instead of doing the performance on the keys. I get to choose where I put my attention, even though I don't always realize it.

Hinch knows exactly what I mean. He nods in agreement as he says, "You want to be present. You want to be still. You want to forget everything that's already happened."

WE ARE ALWAYS AT OUR BEST
WHEN WE ARE NOT THINKING ABOUT OURSELVES

The funny thing is – and it is counterintuitive – we are always at our best when we are not thinking about ourselves. After all, how can you focus on the task at hand when you are considering where you are, or how you're doing? A clear mind is the key to powerful action, at the piano or inside a race car. How about inside your organization? There's a curious connection between self-awareness and self-consciousness. I notice that neither will help me to get out of my own way – and really accelerate my results.

"Humility is not thinking less of yourself, but thinking of yourself less."
—C. S. Lewis, author

"My understanding of momentum is very different from what most people might tell you. Because it's a big part of what I do. On top of the training and the repetition of the dance moves – or the moves on the track, for that matter – power can come from something small. Momentum means that you don't always have to use brute force or a big raw push to execute something really powerful. Sometimes that slow burn is really more effective, a more efficient way to go about it," Hinch tells me.

What about setbacks? Hinch shifts gears and goes back to the track, telling me about "filling the mirrors" of another driver. Filling the mirrors is a tactic that lets the driver in front of you know that you are on his tail, and not going to let up. The maneuver is designed to create distraction – and cause a setback for the other driver.

"At speed, the consequences of every move can be fantastically high. And if somebody does something that affects you in a negative way, it's very hard not to have an emotion creep in, whether it's anger or fear or whatever it is," Hinch explains. Filling the mirrors is an attempt to get into the headspace of the driver in front of you and force some kind of error.

"Never look back. Unless you are planning to go that way."
—Henry David Thoreau, American essayist, poet, and author

So, when people are filling your mirrors, how do you get past that emotional speed bump? How do you avoid letting emotion literally take you off track?

Hinch gets philosophical about the man in the mirror. "I have to see that what just happened didn't happen to me. It just happened."

He's right. When I think about the times in my life that I saw events as personal, taking on blame instead of playing my game, I was never at my best. I saw people and circumstances in my rearview mirror, and reacted from a place of imagination, not acceptance. As the saying goes, it's never tougher than it is in your mind.

So many times, in my career, I was looking in my rearview mirror instead of looking at the track ahead. Rather than concentrating on what I could improve, or where I could move, I was caught up in what I couldn't control. I was assigning stories to the "drivers" around me, making decisions based on reflections instead of reality. I gave in to the tactics and tricks of others, instead of playing my own game – and playing to win.

There's no judgment in watching the rearview mirror – we've all done it. We've all been spooked by objects that may be closer than they appear! But where's the fun in that? Where's the ability to accept, and adapt, if you're responding to a reflection inside your imagination – instead of acting on what's really going on?

A realization hits me at 235 miles per hour: The race car driver says that the key to acceleration is remaining in neutral.

NEUTRAL
IS WHERE THE REAL POWER IS

Neutral is where the real power is.

Consider the situation: you are traveling at 330 feet per second, inside a four-wheeled track missile where you are pinned to your seat every time you make a left turn. The only way to respond to anything and everything is from a place of neutrality.

Acceleration comes from calm. Anything else just leads to calamity.

The actions of the track and the car and the other drivers aren't personal. Emotional journeys take you away from the race you're trying to run. But before we put more blame into the game, let's recognize one important fact: that emotional journey is part of being human! The ups and downs of our thoughts can be a bit of a roller coaster, even when our circumstances have changed very little. Have you been there? When the stakes are high – and you're shifting gears – it's easy to get lost in interpretation, instead of acceptance. Instead of action. But that's not the game that Hinchcliffe wants to play.

When you see that life isn't personal, you're truly becoming a professional. Your understanding will change the game. Eliminate blame. Allow you never to be the same. So that working from anywhere is what you can claim. Take that, Dr. Seuss. But I digress.

I notice:

1. Acceleration starts (and stays) in neutral when we are at our best.
2. Reaction times accelerate when we see that life isn't personal.
3. People are always going to try and fill your mirrors. How you react is always a choice – and that choice is up to you.

Today, Hinchcliffe doesn't look like he's afraid of much of anything. But surely there was some hesitation when he made his comeback into racing? When he went from shish kabob in 2015 to winning the Indianapolis pole position in 2016: was there any reluctance to getting back on the track?

"Honestly, there was no hesitation. None. I looked at it this way: *this thing happened.* It doesn't matter how or why or what caused it; it happened. It's over now, and I can't change that. Spending any energy on that thinking is pointless. So by not thinking of it as 'Oh yeah, I crashed my car on a racetrack,' it gets simpler. It gets truer, without the emotions around it. I just had an accident. When I got back in the car, my brain wasn't any more worried about my body any more than I would have been when I was on the track and getting ready to race."

Hinchcliffe practices being in neutral, so that life's little challenges don't slow him down. How about you? What gear are you in, right now?

How tough is that next turn, when you're busy getting angry with all the other drivers and all the choices they are making?

"This is just temporary. Whatever 'this' is. I don't have to stay here," Hinch shares, recalling the story of his recovery. Routines, whether getting into a race car or getting into physical therapy, signaled a change for him. "There were moments in the hospital where I started thinking, 'I'm not sure I can ever do anything close to driving a race car again, based on how much pain I'm in.' Then another thought showed up. 'Nope, this is just a phase. This time is going to get better. We [his team of doctors and his family] will make this better." And they did.

James Hinchcliffe lives in a world of split-second decisions, where he has seen that momentum isn't about pushing and striving and chasing unnecessary risks. Because, as the saying goes, life is a marathon, not a sprint.

I wonder about that marathon/sprint thing. Is that a philosophy for Indy car racing, or business, or life? James Hinchcliffe looks at me with a smile. He says, simply, "Yes. I think you're starting to see what I'm talking about."

James confides in me. "You can't change what you can't change, Karen. I find a lot of people focus so much energy on things they can't change." He sighs and shakes his head. "And whether that's things that are in the past, which literally nobody can change, or things that are just simply out of their realm of control at a given time or place, people spend too much time and energy on things they cannot control. If they just redirected that energy and brain capacity to whatever elements of the situation they can command, to get the outcome they want, they'd be more successful."

Indeed. One lap at a time.

Game Changers.

What can you do to access true acceleration in your life and your career? Here are some key reminders from James Hinchcliffe that you can implement before your next pit stop.

1. Who is "filling your mirrors"? Do you have a boss, or co-worker, or customer who seems to be crowding you, challenging you, hoping that you will react? It's easy to see situations as sinister. Everybody does it! What happens if you don't fall into that trap – if you design your game so that you see things in a different way? What if what's happening isn't happening to you – it's just happening? How can you see the impersonal side of events around you – and what changes when you do?

2. What's that routine that you go through, to get into the "cockpit" for your work? As we've seen throughout this book, work isn't a place or a time; it's a state of mind. Placing yourself in that mindset often involves a routine, so that you can easily adapt and enter the game with clarity and

precision. How do you get "buckled in" for accessing your best work?

3. What does being in neutral look like for you? Can you see that spending time getting wrapped up in the emotions of a situation will deprive you of the ability to act with clarity? Making split-second decisions and trusting your gut means clearing your mind of the mental chatter that slows down your performance.

4. When Hinchcliffe went on *Dancing with the Stars*, he literally learned some new choreography on his road to recovery. After his accident, he was playing a different game – but the memories of the past didn't keep him from creating a new future. His experience inside a race car informed the way that he took the stage, and foxtrotted his way to the runner-up position. What's the new choreography you're longing to learn, right now? What's the setback that has you primed for a comeback? Just as Hinch found an advocate in his dance partner, who's there to help you to slow down and really listen to the music? Sometimes, when we slow down to go fast, it's easier to play along. In fact, the whole game changes when we see all of the possibilities.

Accept. Adapt. Accelerate.

Don't let life slap you in the face. When you slow down, you can go fast. Get into your routine, and find your way to neutral if you really want to accelerate your results. Because small and incremental improvements are what win the race – not blowing yourself up because of burnout.

Chapter 10.
Rediscovering the Magic

"We keep moving forward, opening new doors and doing new things, because we're curious, and curiosity keeps leading us down new paths. When you're curious, you find lots of interesting things to do."

—Walt Disney

The ticket said it all.

The Happiest Place on Earth. What comes to mind for you? For me, the ticket to Disneyworld was everything childhood Karen ever dreamed of. It was my first airplane ride. My first trip to Florida. My first visit to the Magic Kingdom. And my first big adventure away from my parents. Before I even set foot into the House of Mouse, I began to experience the anticipation and thrill that can only be felt – truly felt – by a child.

I'll never forget the night before the flight, sleeping in one of my grandfather's undershirts as a makeshift nightgown. I could hardly fall asleep, but eventually I went down with the kind of deep sleep that comes to kids who try to outlast their anticipation until the wee hours. Through the deep fog of sleep, my grandpa's voice: "Come on Karen! Let's go – we've got to get you into the car so we make it to the airport on time!"

Where does the magic really come from? They call it the Magic Kingdom for a reason – or was it just a slogan? For me,

I found the magic inside the meaning. In the middle of a sun-showery Florida day, tiny Karen found the origin of the magic. Do you know where it comes from?

A sudden pop-up shower visited Orlando and we dashed over to the line for "It's a Small World." The line was short and before the rainstorm really got going, we were ushered into our boat. The dazzling diorama of mechanized people and places made my eyes unable to blink, for fear I might miss even one moment of the never-ending spectacle. You may laugh to think of those singing dolls right now, and the song that played on an endless loop as the air conditioning hit your face, providing relief from the humidity outside. See it, if you can, through a child's eyes: the singing changes into another language! Dolls in bright costumes smiling and moving in unison! Experiencing that spectacle for the first time, I never wanted it to end.

As soon as we got off the ride, it was pouring down rain. My strategy – yes, I was a kid but I still had a strategy – was to run back to the line. My grandparents, barely keeping up, joined me at the back of the line. They stood by me, so I could ride on "It's a Small World." Because they knew what every parent and grandparent learns, the minute they arrive in Disneyworld: it's all about the kids. And this kid wanted to hit that ride. Over and over and over again. I was the oldest grandchild, and the only one on that trip. And my grandparents were ready to ride!

On our sixth trip past the dancing dolls, the storm crackled and shook the entire ride. A loud boom of thunder overpowered the music, with a long and startling rumble.

The roar grew even louder when the power went out. The music stopped. The boats stopped. The bright lights and sparkling dolls were replaced with a sheet of blackness.

Our boat, like the other boats on the journey, sat in complete and silent darkness. Chatter and conversions quickly pierced the silence, as parents tried to calm themselves, and then their kids. The occasional clap of thunder, followed high-pitched squeals, replaced the sound of that song you know all too well. Quickly, the emergency lights came on – lighting up the mechanical river beneath us. Eerie shadows painted the frozen faces of the unanimated dolls that had once seemed so full of life.

I remember the dark. I remember thinking how different the experience felt.

I was with the same people on the same boat on the same ride. The boat was the same, the robotic miniature dolls were the same. The motion had changed. And so had the lighting. Everything was still there, just frozen in the long shadows of the house lights.

The stop was a shock. When would the ride get moving again? What would have to happen – when would the storm pass? Once the thunder was gone, would they be able to restore the power and get us moving again? Parents in other boats were looking for an engineer or ride operator to come and save the day. But no one came.

I still have several mementos from that childhood visit, if you can believe it. A Mickey magnet. A postcard proclaiming the "32 fabulous shops and restaurants" of the Disney Village. And a book of matches from the Dutch Inn resort hotel – home to 614 fabulous rooms that have long since faded into history. But the one memento that hasn't been affected by time is a beautiful coffee mug, painted with the faces and places of the Disney princesses.

At the bottom of the mug, these words are written in golden yellow: "Remember the magic."

I can never forget it. The magic was more than just a place; it was an experience. An experience that remained with me even when the ride stopped. The same way that everything closed down on or around March 13, 2020.

Everyone was in motion all over the world, speaking all kinds of different languages. Then the ride of life stopped. Shut down, as it were, by a global pandemic – the likes of which no one alive today has ever seen before.

Reluctantly, we were reminded that it's a small world. As we moved into our makeshift home offices, balancing work and school and supervisor deadlines from the kitchen table, the world started to feel very small indeed.

For months, we sat inside this frozen moment. The pandemic moment. The time where all of the movement of the world was put on pause. When would things get moving again? Who or what was going to come out of the darkness and get things started?

On that Small World ride, an engineer eventually appeared from between two Dutch dolls, revealing a hidden doorway that vanished under the darkness of the ride. Under bright lights, we saw the opening clearly and we received an update on a possible timeline. I don't remember what was said, but all of the adults seemed to calm down. What I do remember is that I never let go of the magic. Even when the ride stopped.

Do you remember the magic?

The magic is in the moment we're living in right now. Even if you feel stuck. Even if things have come to a complete stop. Can you remember what it is that really makes the magic? It's not the work of the Imagineers at Disney Studios, or the hidden engineer who finally gets the power back on.

I looked into the eyes of my grandparents. I saw their smiling faces. Things had stopped, but their joy was still there. I felt as though they could keep going on this ride 100 more times – and, truth be told, childhood Karen was already working towards that quota. But the thunderstorm got in the way. Stopped the ride. Halted our game. But it didn't take away the magic.

Because who we surround ourselves with is where the joy really comes from. The excitement of "It's A Small World" didn't come from the constant motion, blinking lights, or unrelenting melody that blasted us, over and over again.

The magic was in the moment of being fully present. Being together. Being on an adventure. And facing the unknown together.

I keep the Mickey magnet on my desk now. As the world comes back into motion, I want to remind myself of the magic. The childlike wonder of possibility – a sense of curiosity that continued, even when the ride had stopped.

Life keeps going, even when it seems like the magic has gone. Nothing has disappeared. The magic has shifted and changed. And we have had to adapt along with those shifts. Now, as we explore new commitments and travel possibilities and different kinds of expectations, I wonder:

Can we remember the magic?

Can we take the best of the pandemic and put it into play, in a new kind of game? Can we acknowledge that we lived in a very small world, as we pause and move into a new blueprint for tomorrow?

The magic isn't out there. The game isn't created by someone else, or reserved for other players. You are the architect of the *Success from Anywhere* blueprint. Remembering the magic isn't some exercise in woo-woo; it's simply a choice. A choice to approach the future with progressive consciousness. With the enthusiasm and excitement that comes when we see that the magic is within our reach. The system is built to adapt, and we are capable of more than we know.

Acceleration is great. But just being present for someone – even when things come to a complete stop – might just be the most magical thing you can do, right now.

The ride restarted. My grandparents were each holding one of my hands. I hadn't even noticed until we started moving again. Their hands, like their support, were always there for me – even when I didn't always see it. I smiled and looked up at them, as the ride came back to life.

The music spooled slowly from a low growl into the chirpy earworm that kids love and adults endure. The lights began to flash and the dolls resumed their dance. We were almost at the end of the ride, and I didn't even know it. When you're in the dark in a place you've never been before (and you don't know how to do your multiplication tables yet), the world can be a very mysterious place. And I found that mystery absolutely magical.

And I still do.

Do you remember how "It's a Small World" came to an end? As the boats leave the Small World for the real one, an announcement over the loudspeaker replaces the unstoppable chorus with valuable instructions. The announcer lets everyone know that the platform and the boat are both moving. The mysterious voice reminds you to proceed with caution, asking parents to take small children firmly by the hand. (If you're amazed that I still remember that announcement after all these years, suffice it to say: I really enjoyed going on that ride. Over and over and over again. I think I can still do some of the doll choreography, but I'll save that for my next tap class.)

Today, the world is moving again. So are we. Depending on where you are when you read (or hear) these words, things may be moving more slowly than you would like. Or perhaps things have accelerated, and you are trying to catch up.

Whatever the case may be, capturing the future of work isn't so much about organizational design as it is designing the Small World that fits for you. Because when the player is successful, the game can change. When you are playing at a new level, you never forget the magic: the magic of adventure, inside the game of life.

A world filled with magic and possibility isn't just a child's dream. There's a choice that you can make, right now, to design magic into your next move.

Whether you're working from home, holding court in a hybrid model, or bringing it all back to the office, be deliberate in the design of your blueprint. Make choices that serve you, and find the way to be true to yourself, remembering who you are, and never losing sight of your values.

If you are successful,

YOUR ORGANIZATION IS SUCCESSFUL

No one can say which business model is right for you, or your company. No one, that is, except you. If you are successful, your organization is successful. Be the architect of what you need, and what your organization needs. The blueprint will help you to play a different game, if you have the courage to do so. Hopefully this book has helped you to become a better player. To become the version of yourself you were meant to be. To find the commitment to your values, five minutes at a time, as you can step out of the pains of the pandemic to find new possibilities.

The rules of your game have not been written. Not by me. Or your mom. Or your boyfriend. Or your boss. The blueprint is up to you.

Pick up your pen. Discover where progressive consciousness will take you. And don't let slaps and setbacks slow you down. Adaptability is built into your DNA, and acceleration is easier than it might seem right now.

The simple fact is this: no one can predict the future. The pandemic may be behind us, but challenges will never disappear. When I wrote this book, I wondered to myself: how can I craft a blueprint that will stand the test of time? A blueprint that pulls us out of the pandemic, and propels us all towards whatever is next?

I realized I couldn't do it.

That's why I need your help. Because I can point and guide and advise and share but at the end of the day, the blueprint is still yours to create. Who knows your values better than you? *Success from Anywhere* isn't just my book. It's yours, and it always has been.

Yours to create.

You know the game you need to be playing. You know the setbacks that are holding you back, better than I ever will. Ready to say, "Thank God that's over"? Ready to accelerate? We are wired to adapt, and to step into a new game.

But creating your own game takes one – and only one – simple step. It takes *action*.

Sometimes the lights will go out. Sometimes we will find ourselves in the dark, yet again. Challenges are part of the game. The good news is that you know how to choose differently. You understand how we are built for growth and expansion. You have the chance to be deliberate – maybe even inspired – about the life that you can create.

Commit to your values, and the values of your organization, so that you can serve at a deeper level. Reach out to others who may be in the dark, or experiencing a panic attack, or facing some other challenge. Let them know that they are not alone. Neither are you, my friend.

There's never been a more important time for us to come together. To connect. To take our experiences and turn them into something new. Something magical. Something that makes you say, "Yes, I want to play in that game!"

The ride is starting again. The music is playing, reminding us of a child's curiosity, energy, and unstoppable creativity. The magic that's inside of you, right now. It's never been quarantined. You can always create a new blueprint. Always.

I just have one question for you. What game are you going to play today?

Acknowledgments.

Now what?

That's the question I asked myself, following the publication of *Working from Home: Making the New Normal Work for You.* The question wasn't in reference to what was next for me personally. The question was in reference to what was next for us *collectively*, as companies, countries, communities, citizens, and colleagues. Who would we become? Who could we become? And how might the new world of work – well, work, post-pandemic?

Amid my conundrum about how to predict the post-pandemic future, I'm grateful Tom Peters reminded me that character is what endures. And hence the framing for this book was born. Tom, you exemplify excellence in every interaction. You are generous with your time, your wisdom, and your kindness. You are extremely human. Thank you for lending your voice to this work. Collaborating with you is the honor of a lifetime.

Thank you to Chef Karl Benko for curating a course about excellence for me as a culinary student and as an intern. Reminiscing with you about our experience reminded me there is no excellence without education and execution. To Alessia Bell, from Principles, a Ray Dalio Company – thank you for your input and support.

Excellence is an extension of trust. Thank you to David Horsager for sharing your expertise about trust amidst a busy book launch of your own.

I defy you to find a more trusted, excellent leader than my boss, Bruce Richardson. Thank you for providing me with a continuous supply of research and resounding encouragement. Your friendship is a gift that encourages me to live to my highest potential.

Thank you to James Hinchcliffe for putting our readers and me in the driver's seat of discovery. Your lessons learned reveal game-winning strategies we can all deploy to maneuver through life with speed, precision, and accuracy.

I'm unlikely to appear on *Dancing with the Stars* like James Hinchcliffe did. Which is why I'm especially grateful to my tap-dancing instructor, the ever-encouraging Gabby, for making me feel like a star. You've choreographed more fun into my life than you may know.

Friends of authors enjoy the occasional misfortune of appearing in print. Thanks to Kate, Rodney, and Dee for your enduring friendship and for many memorable moments through the years. And to Eric, HRH, and BDJ for living through book after book and for pretending to believe me when I say, "I'm never doing this again." I am grateful.

The person who teaches me unexpected strategies to better navigate the game of life is my brother, Paul. We've come a long way from "The Barn," and we're both better for it. If we weren't related, I would choose you as a friend. May your whole life be like a convertible cruise down the A1A.

To my favorite CEOs, Fitch and Janna, thank you for sharing your big imagination and even bigger hearts with me. I hope every reader subscribes to your candy service, and we make the world a little bit sweeter for everyone. Yes, I promise to bring the Nerf gun you sent for our next visit. (I just need more practice, and, possibly, body armor.) Tell your parents thanks for allowing me to put you in print and also that I said you could have two desserts after dinner tonight. (You're welcome).

Thank you to Chris Westfall for inviting me to step into a new kind of freedom. Freedom from expectations in favor of experiences. Freedom from deadlines in favor of discoveries. Freedom from the past in favor of potential. As my story has evolved through the years, I'm grateful you are the constant in my narrative. You always have a new lesson to share that's the one I need to learn at any given moment. Thank you for teaching me a new definition of what it means to live. It's (I fight the urge to edit this) . . . *easier*.

Thank you to Jeanenne Ray, Sally Baker, Dawn Kilgore, and the team at Wiley for moving mountains. Three books in 18 months is an incredible climb. Thanks for making another summit possible. To John Taschek, Dan Farber, David Simon, and Mathew Sweezey at Salesforce: I appreciate your enduring support and wisdom more than you know.

Finally, to all my readers, may you design your game your way. Success is not a location, or a timeframe, it's a state of mind. Maybe even a state of play, when you see new possibilities ahead. May you rewrite the rules in your own way. And may you delight in playing to win, at the game that matters most: the game of life.

— Karen Mangia

About the Author

Karen Mangia is Vice President of Customer and Market Insights at Salesforce. Her work focuses on strategies for personal and professional success, and she regularly works with executives, managers and future leaders at companies around the globe. She is the author of *Listen Up!* and *Working from Home: Making the New Normal Work for You* (Wiley). She has been featured in *Forbes* and regularly writes for Thrive Global and ZDNet. Committed to diversity and inclusion, she serves on her company's Work from Home Taskforce and the Racial Equality and Justice Task Force. She is a TEDx speaker and the author of *Success With Less* (Marie Street Press), a book that chronicles her own personal journey through a life-threatening health crisis. Her high-impact keynotes help organizations to access the future of work via innovative insights around the voice of the customer. Find her online at http://karenmangia.com or connect via twitter @karenmangia.

Index